THE WISDOM *of*
the LOTUS SUTRA

THE WISDOM OF THE
LOTUS SUTRA
A DISCUSSION

VOLUME I

EXAMINING CHAPTERS 1–2:
INTRODUCTION
EXPEDIENT MEANS

Daisaku Ikeda
Katsuji Saito • Takanori Endo • Haruo Suda

World Tribune
Press

Published by
World Tribune Press
606 Wilshire Blvd.,
Santa Monica, CA 90401

ISBN 0-915678-69-1

Design by Gopa Design
Cover image © Photodisc

10 9 8 7 6 5 4 3 2

Publisher's Cataloging-in-Publication
(Provided by Quality Books, Inc.)

The Wisdom of the Lotus Sutra. Volume 1 :
   a discussion : examining chapters 1-2 /
   Daisaku Ikeda… [et al]. — 1st ed.
      p. cm.
      Includes index.
      ISBN: 0-915678-69-1

      1. Tripitaka. Sutrapitaka.
Saddharmapundarikasutra — Criticism,
interpretation, etc. 2. Nichiren, 1222-1282 —
Teachings. I. Ikeda, Daisaku.

BQ2057.W57 2000   294.3'85
                  QB199-500560

Table of Contents

Foreword

Foreword

"The Lotus Sutra teaches of the great hidden treasure of the heart, as vast as the universe itself, which dispels any feelings of powerlessness," writes SGI President Ikeda. "It teaches a dynamic way of living in which we breathe the immense life of the universe itself. It teaches the true great adventure of self-reformation."

Indeed, the Lotus Sutra is a profound teaching, the basis of Nichiren Daishonin's Buddhism and our faith. Though it plays such a central role in our beliefs, honestly speaking I have long had a difficult time understanding it completely. Thanks to this dialogue, however, the Lotus Sutra has come alive for me, and I am understanding it more than ever. President Ikeda and the others so clearly elucidate the important principles and apply them to life, society and our own SGI activities. No longer is it only a centuries-old work but a living, breathing manual for finding happiness and fulfillment today.

One of the concepts for which I got a much deeper appreciation was the Bodhisattvas of the Earth. For instance, President Ikeda says:

> The compassion of the universe is the function inherently possessed by the Buddha. It is also the function of the inherent world of Bodhisattva, the power of the Bodhisattvas of the Earth. Therefore, in a general sense, all living things in the universe are sacred Bodhisattvas of the Earth; whereas in a specific sense, Bodhisattvas of the Earth refer to those who have awakened to this law of life. The path of the bodhisattva lies in supremely

humane action. And such action, fundamentally, is at one with the function of compassion of the universe. When we pray, speak out and take action for the happiness of a friend, the eternal life of the universe manifests through our thoughts, words and deeds.

Diamonds like this make this work an indispensable companion to the Lotus Sutra. Each chapter contains new inspiration, fuel for greater awakening and the philosophical basis for our movement of peace, culture and education. By providing such a clear direction for humanity and a clear exposition of the wisdom contained in this sutra, I feel that this work, to be completed in six volumes, could be looked upon as a Lotus Sutra of the twenty-first century.

I hope that all readers will thoroughly study and thoroughly enjoy this new series of books and will strive together to manifest these ideals so that we can further our efforts for the peace and happiness of all humankind.

Daniel Nagashima
SGI-USA General Director

Editor's Note

This book is a series of discussions among SGI President Daisaku Ikeda, Soka Gakkai Study Department Chief Katsuji Saito and vice chiefs Takanori Endo and Haruo Suda. It was first serialized in English starting with the April 1995 issue of *Seikyo Times* (now *Living Buddhism*).

The following abbreviations appear in some citations:

✦ WND, page number(s) — refers to *The Writings of Nichiren Daishonin* (Soka Gakkai: Tokyo; 1999)

✦ GZ, page number(s) — refers to the *Gosho Zenshu*, the Japanese-language compilation of letters, treatises, essays and oral teachings of Nichiren Daishonin.

✦ LS(chapter number), page number(s) — refers to *The Lotus Sutra*, translated by Burton Watson (Columbia University Press: New York; 1993)

PART ONE

Prologue

1 Surmounting the Absence of Philosophy in Our Age

Daisaku Ikeda: Now is the time to engage in an earnest discussion of religion's role in the next century. With the collapse of communism and a pervasive absence of philosophy in our age, humanity is now searching beyond the present for a powerful new philosophy. People are searching for something that will satisfy the spiritual emptiness they feel, something that will revive their weary lives and fill them once again with hope and vigor. Humanity is searching for the wisdom that will provide true direction and purpose to the individual and society.

Whether it be the war-torn states of the former Yugoslavia, the affluent industrialized nations, the disordered former socialist states or the poverty-stricken Third World, humanity is beginning to recognize that something is wrong with the world today, when economic growth is viewed as the supreme imperative. We are starting to recognize that people must come first and that human growth may be what is most important. We are coming to understand that, in our information-oriented societies with their explosion of knowledge, we urgently need a matching explosion of wisdom to use that knowledge properly.

Something is wrong. Something is missing. Scientific developments alone cannot bring happiness. Neither socialism nor capitalism can save us. No matter how many conferences we hold, how we stress ethics and morality or lecture on human psychology or philosophy, something essential is lacking. This, I believe, is a fair description of humanity's present state of mind.

French author Antoine de Saint-Exupéry, well known for his book *The Little Prince*, writes:

> We have to understand that somewhere along the way we have taken the wrong road. Humanity as a whole is richer than ever before. We enjoy unsurpassed affluence and leisure time. Yet something more basic, something indefinable, is lacking. The sensation of ourselves as human beings becomes gradually more and more rare. We have lost something that was one of our mysterious prerogatives.[1]

Humanity has taken the wrong road, he says. Where are we going and for what purpose?

This question reminds me of a famous scene in the Lotus Sutra. When the multitude of bodhisattvas appears out of the earth in the "Emerging from the Earth" chapter, the bodhisattva Maitreya asks Shakyamuni to explain

> where they have come from,
> what causes and conditions bring them together! (LS15, 216)

Maitreya asks this as a representative of all who are assembled.

Katsuji Saito: Shakyamuni praises Maitreya for asking such an important question. And in reply, Shakyamuni preaches the most important teaching of the entire Lotus Sutra, which is contained in "The Life Span of the Thus Come One" [hereafter referred to as the "Life Span"] chapter.

Ikeda: Maitreya's query is indeed important. I'd like to discuss its significance from a doctrinal perspective on another occasion. Put quite simply, however, it comes down to the questions: Where have we come from? For what purpose were we born in this world?

Takanori Endo: I am reminded of the impromptu poem you recited before [the second Soka Gakkai president] Josei Toda at the first Gakkai discussion meeting you attended as a young man. This scene is recounted in *The Human Revolution.*

> *Traveler,*
> *Where do you come from?*
> *And where do you go?*
> *The moon has set,*
> *And the sun has not yet risen.*
> *In the darkness before dawn*
> *I advance*
> *In search of light.*
> *To dispel the dark clouds in my mind*
> *To seek a great tree unbowed by the storm,*
> *I spring from the earth.*[2]

Ikeda: As a young person struggling amid the chaos of postwar Japan, I was trying earnestly to find the meaning of life. Then I met Mr. Toda. Here was a man who had been imprisoned for his opposition to the Japanese militarist government [during World War II]. Instinctively, I felt I could trust him. My encounter with Mr. Toda was my encounter with the Lotus Sutra. All human endeavor is inspired by the effort to answer the questions: Where do we come from? Where we are going? Why we are here?

Haruo Suda: The issue then becomes what philosophy, religion or belief system can provide clear answers to those questions. Though an entire nation may have been reduced to ashes by war, its people's future will remain bright as long as a positive philosophy still pulses in their hearts.

Saito: That is also the philosophy of the Lotus Sutra.

Suda: On the other hand, if people's hearts are laid to waste, their future will be dark even if they live in an affluent society.

Ikeda: Precisely. I am reminded of the words of Austrian psychologist Viktor Frankl, who, describing the contemporary state of mind, said that "our hearts have been bombed."[3] Dr. Frankl is well known for surviving imprisonment in a World War II Nazi concentration camp.

Endo: Yes, and he wrote a famous book about that experience.

Ikeda: Dr. Frankl writes: "The abuse of every kind of passion has resulted in an age in which all types of idealism have been destroyed. While we would normally expect to find the younger generation extremely passionate and idealistic, today's generation, today's youth, have no ideals at all."[4] Dr. Frankl is saying that young people have lost the meaning of living.

Endo: The concentration camps were the epitome of an environment that completely destroyed all human dignity and meaning in life. Yet even there some survived, maintaining their humanity throughout the ordeal.

Dr. Frankl is suggesting, I think, that even though the concentration camps have been destroyed and the war is over, humanity remains locked up in a sort of invisible concentration camp.

Ikeda: Yes, you may be right. Some say the prevailing mood in the world today is one of powerlessness. Whatever the case may be, we are all aware that things cannot continue as they are. Yet decisions about political, economic and environmental issues all seem to be made somewhere beyond our reach. What can the individual accomplish in the face of the huge institutions that run our world? This feeling of powerlessness fuels a vicious cycle that only worsens the situation and increases people's sense of futility.

At the opposite extreme of this sense of powerlessness lie the Lotus Sutra's philosophy of 'three thousand realms in a single moment of life' and the application of this teaching to our daily lives. This principle teaches us that the inner determination of an individual can transform everything; it gives ultimate expression to the infinite potential and dignity inherent in each human life.

Saito: We need to emphasize that the human being is not pitiful and powerless. Russian politician Aleksandr Yakovlev is often called the architect of the former Soviet Union's policy of perestroika. In response to the question, "Does Russia have a future?" he writes: "Today, even the most objective scientific rationalism teaches us that the human race faces certain destruction unless we recognize the value of every individual."[5]

Ikeda: I last met Dr. Yakovlev in May 1994 in Moscow. He earnestly seeks the advent of a "Russian renaissance" centering on a restoration of human values. He has said:

> In the few remaining years of the twentieth century, the last illusions of the communism that we have known from the mid-nineteenth century will have been utterly destroyed. That is certain. At the same time, we will see a restoration of truly humane values. Until now, humane values have been, as a matter of active policy, completely overwhelmed by misunderstanding, lies and slander. Finally the time when they will be liberated has come. When we consider both the present and the future, we cannot escape the conclusion that the greatest crisis we face today is in the realm of spiritual ideals.[6]

Saito: The Lotus Sutra constitutes the grandest and most sublime presentation of those humane values.

Ikeda: Yes, that is our firm conviction. There was a period in the history of the Holy Roman Empire called the Great Interregnum (1254–73). During that period the empire's throne was vacant for all practical purposes. Interestingly, this coincides with the period in which Nichiren Daishonin lived.

Today, after the Cold War, we are living in a "Great Interregnum of Philosophy," an era in which there is an absence of any guiding philosophy. That is why this is precisely the time to speak of the Lotus Sutra, long known as the king of sutras.

Endo: The Lotus Sutra is the king and champion of all sutras. I fully agree we live in a Great Interregnum today in terms of philosophy. Faith in communism has disappeared, yet it is doubtful whether the newfound freedom of those liberated from its yoke really makes them happy. Instead, the worship of money, shallow materialism and mindless pleasure-seeking have spread across the globe.

Suda: I agree. President Václav Havel of the Czech Republic is renowned as a staunch campaigner against the oppression of the communist state. Mr. Havel warns of the changes that have been taking place in society after the liberation from communism: "The return of freedom to a society that was morally unhinged has produced...an enormous and dazzling explosion of every imaginable human vice.... We are witness to a bizarre state of affairs: society has freed itself, true, but in some ways it behaves worse than when it was in chains...."[7]

Saito: Extreme nationalism is one of those vices. In unified Germany, for example, even though the neo-Nazi movement has only an extremely small number of supporters, calls for the exclusion of certain races are growing among the general populace. Some Germans even say the Berlin Wall should be rebuilt—but this time around the entire country, to keep foreigners out.

Ikeda: Yes, the roots of racism run deep. Movements to fan racial hatred for political, economic or religious advantage are always with us. The seriousness of this problem lies in that it is so closely tied to people's spiritual and emotional desires. In other words, we might say the desire for an identity—to know where one came from and where one is going—lies at the root of racism. People cannot withstand a vacuum of ideas; a philosophical and ideological void drives people to seek their identity in their race.

That, of course, is one reason religion is important, but in reality religion often contributes to divisiveness.

Endo: Yasushi Akashi, special representative of the United Nations secretary-general assigned to the task of finding an end to the conflict in the former Yugoslavia, had this to say at the Sixth World Conference on Religion and Peace [November 1994]: "In the former republic of Yugoslavia, religion was appropriated and misused by intolerant racists. If religious leaders had been on the ball and had stood up before the conflict reached this stage, war could have been avoided."[8]

Ikeda: Mr. Akashi is a valued friend of mine. The war in the former Yugoslavia is a terrible tragedy. When I think of the people there, my heart breaks. Their country has become a living hell. One Bosnian poet commented: "The only things we can write in Sarajevo today are obituaries."[9]

Saito: I have heard that when Orthodox Christian soldiers of the Serbian forces take Roman Catholic Croatian soldiers prisoner, they force them to perform the sign of the cross with three fingers, in the Orthodox fashion.

Suda: The Roman Catholic practice uses two fingers.

Saito: Yes. I have heard that if the prisoners refuse, their captors bind their fingers together with wire so that they cannot help but perform the sign of the cross with three fingers. Whether or not this is true, pictures of these prisoners are printed in Croatian newspapers. When Croatians see them, of course, their hatred for the Serbs is only fanned.[10]

Ikeda: Depending on the use to which it is put, religion can be a demonic force. Religion should bring us together, but it is exploited by some to create greater schisms among us. Nothing could be more unfortunate.

Religion must always be for the people. People do not exist for the sake of religion. This must be the fundamental guideline of religion in the twenty-first century.

Endo: Dr. Anatoly Logunov, the renowned Russian physicist and former rector of Moscow State University, says that one lesson he learned from you, Mr. Ikeda, is that society exists for people and not the other way around. In the Soviet society of the past, he says, that was a shocking idea, because it represented a revival of humane values.

Ikeda: Such emphasis on the human being is the teaching of the Lotus Sutra; it is Buddhist humanism.

We hear stories of the innocents of Sarajevo. One little girl was unable to leave her house for a year and a half. Amid the continuous shelling, even her own room was too dangerous to enter. The toilet and hallway were the safest parts of the house, and she once spent an entire month confined to this space. She had no running water, no electricity. Pieces of bodies blown apart by shell explosions lay strewn about her. In winter, temperatures dropped to −63 degrees F; she had neither wood nor a stove to burn it in. It was so cold that any water she had froze. She couldn't wash her face or hands. A trip to a public well would expose her to the peril of sniper fire.[11]

A seventeen-year-old living under similar conditions writes: "I had many dreams, but the war robbed me of all of them.... I don't know when it will be, but if I can love someone, if I still have the ability within myself, I would like to love someone. The most important thing, no matter what happens, is to be a human being, to remain a human being."[12]

Peace must be a central premise in any discussion of the twenty-first century. Nothing is of any use without peace. That is one reason why religion in the twenty-first century must be a force for the creation of peace. Dr. Johan Galtung, the pioneering Norwegian peace researcher, has concluded that Buddhism is the most pacifistic religion. And the very essence of Buddhism is, of course, the Lotus Sutra.

Endo: The youth's fervent desire to remain human under such desperate circumstances is profoundly moving. As far as appearances are concerned, Japan seems a peaceful country. But I think I am not the only one who has grave doubts as to whether we Japanese have maintained our humanity.

Ikeda: Yes. And that is precisely why, wherever we are, it is necessary to begin with the revitalization of individual human beings. That is what we mean by the reformation of society and the world through human revolution. That is the teaching of the Lotus Sutra. And actions directed toward that end, I would like to stress, represent the wisdom of the Lotus Sutra.

Suda: Even a general overview of society reveals that we live in a period of great upheaval, a time of chaos—a "Great Interregnum of Philosophy" in which old systems of belief have reached a dead end. The world is becoming smaller and smaller, yet we know less and less in what direction to move. It is only natural that humanity today needs a basic standard to guide and lead it.

Ikeda: Actually, the Lotus Sutra is a scripture that shows its true brilliance in just such periods of great transition. The age in which the Lotus Sutra was first taught seems to have been similar.

In Shakyamuni's India, the growth of cities began transcending the old tribal divisions, leading to a new age in which people would form new relationships and have to coexist symbiotically. It was a

time of great intellectual confusion, with people espousing everything from pure materialism to hedonism to asceticism.

Suda: These are among the doctrines of the 'six non-Buddhist
teachers.'[13]

Ikeda: Yes. To bring humanity together in this period of great change,
Shakyamuni taught new principles of integration. And the Lotus
Sutra is the living essence of that teaching.

Later in China and Japan, when religion was in chaos and people didn't know what to believe, the Great Teacher T'ien-t'ai and
Nichiren Daishonin advocated the Lotus Sutra's teachings and
with it boldly confronted the issues of their respective eras and
societies. The Lotus Sutra, one might say, represented the banner
of unity with which they charged ahead in their struggles amid
periods of great spiritual turbulence.

Suda: That reminds me of remarks made by Professor George Tanabe, chairman of the Department of Religion at the University
of Hawaii. The department he heads is known around the world
for its comparative studies of Eastern and Western religions.

In a recent interview with the *Seikyo Shimbun,* the Soka Gakkai
daily newspaper, Dr. Tanabe stated that as a doctrine of the universal
and the eternal, the Lotus Sutra holds an unrivaled place in the
Buddhist canon. We could learn much, he said, by looking into why
the Lotus Sutra has been "so successful in speaking to and having
meaning for so many different people, in so many different places,
so many different cultures and so many different times." The 'one
vehicle' of the Lotus Sutra, Dr. Tanabe stressed, should be understood as meaning that it embraces all other vehicles, all other ways.

This, he said, offers a very important message for people today,
namely, that "we live in one world, on one planet and are really
one people." He was of the opinion that the Lotus Sutra is a universal text for all people that readily can be translated into different cultural contexts.

Ikeda: This is indeed an astute assessment of the contemporary significance of the Lotus Sutra. The Lotus Sutra—"the scripture of the lotus blossom of the Law," as its Japanese name indicates—is the king of sutras. A king does not negate the existence of others; his role is to bring out the full potential of all. Nichiren Daishonin writes:

> Ultimately, all phenomena are contained within one's life, down to the last particle of dust. The nine mountains and the eight seas are encompassed in one's body, and the sun, moon, and myriad stars are found in one's life. We, however, are like a blind person who is incapable of seeing the images reflected in a mirror, or like an infant who has no fear of water or fire. The teachings such as those of the non-Buddhist writings and those of the Hinayana and provisional Mahayana Buddhist scriptures all partially explain the phenomena inherent in one's life. They do not explain them as the Lotus Sutra does. Thus, among the sutras, there are both superior and inferior, and among people also, sages and worthies may be distinguished. (WND, 629)

All philosophies other than the Lotus Sutra are fragments, expressing nothing more than a partial view of the great law of life. Basing ourselves on such fragments, even though they may contain partial truths, will not enable us to realize a thoroughgoing revitalization of our lives. Indeed, philosophies that expound only partial truths end up distorting our lives. The Lotus Sutra, on the other hand, teaches the one fundamental Law that unifies all these fragmentary teachings, gives them proper perspective, and allows each to shine and fulfill its function within the whole. That is the wisdom of the Lotus Sutra.

In the "Life Span" chapter, we find mention of "a skilled physician who is wise and understanding" (LS16, 227). Like a skilled doctor, the wisdom of the Lotus Sutra saves those who are suffering and in pain.

Endo: Later the sutra says of those saved by this wisdom: "Constantly harboring such feelings of grief, they at last come to their senses…" (LS16, 229). What exactly is the wisdom that enabled them to do so?

Ikeda: If there was an easy answer to your question, we'd have no need for this discussion! However, to cut to the conclusion, "they at last come to their senses" means that they finally awoke to the truth that each of them has always been a Buddha from the eternal past and will always be a Buddha into the eternal future. Of course, this realization is not a sudden, simple "Oh, I see."

The Lotus Sutra is an attempt to teach this truth to all in an easily comprehensible fashion. Nichiren Daishonin, the votary of the Lotus Sutra in the Latter Day of the Law,[14] made it possible for all to embody this truth in their daily lives. The Lotus Sutra teaches of the great hidden treasure of the heart, as vast as the universe itself, which dispels any feelings of powerlessness. It teaches a dynamic way of living in which we breathe the immense life of the universe itself. It teaches the true great adventure of self-reformation.

The Lotus Sutra has the breadth and scope to embrace all people on the way to peace. It has the fragrance of magnificent culture and art. It leads us to an unsurpassed state of life imbued with the qualities of eternity, happiness, true self and purity,[15] so that wherever we are, we may say, "This, my land, remains safe and tranquil" (LS16, 230).

The Lotus Sutra has the drama of fighting for justice against evil. It has a warmth that comforts the weary. It has a vibrant, pulsing courage that drives away fear. It has a chorus of joy at attaining absolute freedom throughout past, present and future. It has the soaring flight of liberty. It has brilliant light, flowers, greenery, music, paintings, vivid stories. It offers unsurpassed lessons on psychology, the workings of the human heart; lessons on life; lessons on happiness; and lessons on peace. It maps out the basic rules for good health. It awakens us to the universal truth that a change in one's heart can transform everything.

It is neither the parched desert of individualism nor the prison of totalitarianism; it has the power to manifest a pure land of compassion, in which people complement and encourage one another.

Both communism and capitalism have used people as means for their own ends. But in the Lotus Sutra — the king of sutras — we find a fundamental humanism in which people are the goal and purpose, in which they are both protagonist and sovereign. Perhaps we could call this teaching of the Lotus Sutra a "cosmic humanism."

Saito: Yes, I agree. I think we can draw a clear distinction between cosmic humanism and anthropocentrism — a human-centered view of the universe — which has dominated until now and to which many other life forms have been sacrificed.

Ikeda: I think it is a lofty and powerful designation that will serve as a standard for the twenty-first century. In any case, wisdom and acquiring wisdom are important. We will discuss the relationship between wisdom and knowledge in later chapters, but a British author once wrote: "It is better to have wisdom without learning, than learning without wisdom; just as it is better to be rich without being the possessor of a mine, than to be the possessor of a mine without being rich."[16]

Of course, it is ideal to possess both wisdom and knowledge, but everything ultimately depends on wisdom. Our goal is happiness, and happiness cannot be attained through knowledge alone. The only way to realize true human happiness and prosperity in the twenty-first century, therefore, is to make it a century of wisdom.

Though knowledge can be transmitted from one person to another, wisdom cannot. The only way to develop wisdom is to acquire it through personal experience. That is one reason the Lotus Sutra places such strong emphasis on the teacher–disciple relationship — a relationship in which both parties involve themselves wholly, with every facet of their being.

Endo: Our relationship with the Buddhist scriptures must also be one of total engagement; it is not just an intellectual relationship. This principle also applies to how we live.

Suda: The awakening President Toda attained during his imprisonment was also a result of his desperate quest for the essence of the Lotus Sutra.

Saito: His realization that "the Buddha is life itself" became the starting point for the contemporary revitalization of the Lotus Sutra, which many regarded as merely an ancient text with no practical relevance to the present day. That realization is, I believe, the profound and eternal foundation of the SGI.

Ikeda: I agree. In the next chapter, let's begin by considering the significance of Mr. Toda's enlightenment to the essence of the Lotus Sutra. How should we read the Lotus Sutra? In the "Record of the Orally Transmitted Teachings," Nichiren Daishonin says: "'This is what I heard' means to listen to the meaning and significance of each passage and phrase of the twenty-eight chapters as a teaching that expounds the reality of one's own life. That which is 'heard' is Nam-myoho-renge-kyo" (GZ, 794).

Each passage and phrase of the Lotus Sutra is teaching about oneself, the entity of the Mystic Law. The sutra is not discussing something far removed from our own lives.

In the "Record of the Orally Transmitted Teachings," the Daishonin instructs us how to read the Lotus Sutra from that fundamental standpoint. Deeply and carefully studying the "Orally Transmitted Teachings" with the assistance of your sharp young minds, let us begin this challenging journey to explore the wisdom of the Lotus Sutra for the coming age. It is a journey to the truth that we ourselves are Buddhas. Life is an endless odyssey into the innermost sanctum of our own lives.

German author and poet Hermann Hesse advocated the need for a revolution in consciousness. He was keenly aware of this century's malaise. His poem "Bücher" (Books) is instructive in our exploration of the Lotus Sutra:

All the books in the world
Will not bring you happiness,
But they will quietly lead you
Back inside yourself.

There you will find all you need,
Sun, stars and moon,
For the light for which you search
Dwells within you.

The wisdom you so long sought
In books,
Will then shine forth from every page —
For now that wisdom has become your own.[17]

Saito: In these discussions, we hope to study the Lotus Sutra from various perspectives. Indeed, it is imperative that we do so. Through our diligent studies, we hope to strengthen our conviction that the Lotus Sutra is the core philosophy for twenty-first century leaders.

NOTES

1. Translated from Japanese: Antoine de Saint-Exupéry, *Jinsei ni Imi wo,* trans. Kazutami Watanabi (Tokyo: Misuzu Shobo, 1987) p. 173.

2. Daisaku Ikeda, *The Human Revolution* (New York: Weatherhill, 1986), vol. 1, pp. 217–18.

3. Translated from Japanese: Victor E. Frankl, *Soredemo Jinsei ni Iesu to Iu,* trans. Kunio Yamada and Mike Matsuda (Tokyo: Shunjusha, 1993), p. 7, cf. V.E. Frankl, ... Trotzdem Ja zum Leben sagen (... Still Say Yes to Life) (Wien: Franz Deuticke, 1947).

4. Ibid., p. 10.

5. Translated from Japanese: Aleksandr N. Yakovlev, *Rekishi no Gen'ei* (Illusions of History), trans. Koji Hitachi (Tokyo: Nihon Kezai Shimbunsha, 1993), p. 364.

6. Ibid., p. 378.

7. Václav Havel, *Summer Meditations*, trans. Paul Wilson (New York: Alfred A. Knopf, 1992), pp. 1–2.

8. *Tokyo Shimbun* (Tokyo Newspaper), Nov. 17, 1994.

9. Translated from Japanese: Juan Goytisolo, *Saraevo Nooto* (Guaderno de Sarajevo), trans. Yoshiko Yamamichi (Tokyo: Misuzu Shobo, 1994), p. 114.

10. Kyoko Gendatsu and Eiji Inagawa, *Ushinawareta Shishunki* (Lost Adolescence: Messages from Sarajevo) (Tokyo: Michi Shobo, 1994), p. 62.

11. Ibid., pp. 96–98.

12. Ibid., pp. 272–73.

13. Six non-Buddhist teachers: Influential thinkers in India during Shakyamuni's lifetime who openly broke with the old Vedic tradition and challenged Brahman authority in the Indian social order.

14. Latter Day of the Law: The last of the three periods following Shakyamuni's death, when Buddhism falls into confusion and Shakyamuni's teachings lose the power to lead people to enlightenment. It is said to correspond to the present age.

15. Eternity, happiness, true self, purity: The 'four virtues' or noble qualities of the Buddha's life, expounded in the Nirvana Sutra. Because common mortals possess the Buddha nature, they too can develop these four virtues when they attain Buddhahood by fulfilling the Buddha's teaching.

16. C.C. Colton, *Lacon: Many Things in Few Words* (London: Longman, Rees, Orme, Brown and Green, 1829), vol. 2, p. 18.

17. Translated from German: Hermann Hesse, "Bücher" (Books), *Trost de Nacht: Neue Gedichte von Hermann Hesse* (Berlin: G. Fischer), p. 60.

2   Making the Coming Age
an Age of Life

Saito: The recent devastating earthquake [January 17, 1995] in the Kobe–Osaka area of Japan served as a painful reminder of the preciousness of life. In particular, the Japanese government has drawn anger and outrage from around the world for the slowness and lack of compassion displayed in responding to the disaster. People can't understand why the government didn't make saving lives its top priority.

Ikeda: When I think of the earthquake victims, it really breaks my heart. Day after day the media blared, "More than five thousand dead!" But you can't measure the value of human life by numbers alone. It is not a tragedy simply because more than five thousand people died but because each of those people was irreplaceable and precious — someone's father, mother, child, relative or friend. [It was later determined that more than six thousand perished in the disaster.]

   When my mentor, Josei Toda, was twenty-three, he lost his three-year-old daughter. Recalling that time during a question-and-answer session thirty years later, he said: "I wept the whole night through, lying there with her cold little body in my embrace.... Nothing has ever compared to the grief I felt then." Even relating this story so many years later, he wept. He also confided:

> At that time I thought, "What if my wife were to die?" and I wept harder. Some time later, she did in fact die.

Next, I thought, "What if my mother should die?" I really loved my mother. Then I took it one step further: "What if I were to die?" When I asked myself this question, my whole body shook with terror....

Then I was put in prison, and after reading the Buddhist scriptures, I found the answer to my fears; I understood death at last—though it took me more than twenty years.

I had wept over the death of my child and feared my wife's death as well as my own. Only by finding the answer to the questions of life and death could I become the president of the Soka Gakkai.

Getting back to your original point, how a nation handles a disaster says much about its culture. Emergencies reveal whether a country values human life.

Saito: We must work to create an age in which life is given supreme value.

Ikeda: To achieve that, it is absolutely vital for us to have a philosophy that reveals the wonder, dignity and infinite potential of life. I mentioned the episode about President Toda reading the Lotus Sutra in prison because the ensuing enlightenment he attained there brings the discussion of life into focus.

Suda: In this chapter we'd like to discuss with you the significance of Mr. Toda's enlightenment in prison.

Endo: I was a high school student when I first read about Mr. Toda's profound realization in "The Garden of Life," a chapter in President Ikeda's *The Human Revolution*, then being serialized in the *Seikyo Shimbun.* The work portrays the solemn drama of Mr. Toda's passionate quest for the essence of the Lotus Sutra's teachings while in prison during World War II. Although I knew almost nothing then about the Lotus Sutra, Mr. Toda's odyssey deeply impressed me.

Ikeda: Very simply, Mr. Toda's enlightenment should be remembered as the moment that clearly revealed the Soka Gakkai as the true heir to the Daishonin's Buddhism. That was the starting point of all our propagation activities and our development today, and I firmly believe it was an epoch-making event in the history of Buddhism. Mr. Toda revived Buddhism in contemporary times and made it accessible to all.

When I was younger, Mr. Toda told me about his profound experience in prison. His words left me convinced that his realization formed the religious and philosophical core of the Soka Gakkai. The truth to which he became enlightened is identical to the ultimate teaching of Nichiren Daishonin's Buddhism. I believe Mr. Toda's realization opened a path out of the deadlock facing humanity. Our mission as his disciples is to extend that path in all directions and on all planes.

Suda: This drama began on New Year's Day 1944, when Mr. Toda, imprisoned by militarist authorities, decided to read the entire Lotus Sutra. He firmly resolved to master its meaning completely. Before that, he had tried to send his copy of the Lotus Sutra home a number of times, but somehow it always made its way back to his cell.

Mr. Toda's copy, which also contained the sutras regarded as its introduction and conclusion, was a Chinese text without any of the Japanese punctuation or explanations that would have made it easier to read. Nor did he have access to any of the commentaries written by the Great Teacher T'ien-t'ai or other Buddhist scholars. Moreover, he found himself in the most deplorable of conditions—in prison during wartime. With prayer beads he had fashioned out of cardboard milk-bottle caps, he chanted more than ten thousand daimoku each day. He challenged himself with the full force of his being to understand the Lotus Sutra.

Endo: By early March, he had already read the entire text three times and had just begun reading it again. Then, pondering the meaning of a difficult passage in the Sutra of Immeasurable Meanings, an introduction to the Lotus Sutra, he suddenly realized that the Buddha is life itself.

Ikeda: That was the moment when Buddhism was revived in the twentieth century.

Endo: A verse portion of the Sutra of Immeasurable Meanings containing thirty-four negations[1] begins with the following lines:

> *His body neither existing nor not existing,*
> *neither caused nor conditioned, neither self nor other....*

Ikeda: In context, we know that "his body" refers to the body of the Buddha. But understanding what that really means is another matter altogether. It is something that can only be described by a series of negations, something that does not fit any definition. Yet, no matter how many negatives one uses to describe it, its existence is indisputable.

To say, therefore, that it merely transcends the power of language, that it is unfathomable or dwells in the state of nonsubstantiality (*ku*), thus elevating the Buddha into some transcendent being, does not help our understanding in the least. Mr. Toda wanted to actually perceive this entity. He wanted to experience it with his whole life. He was never satisfied with abstract, conceptual understanding.

Saito: Mr. Toda's state of life at that time is vividly described through the experience of Mr. Gan, the protagonist of his autobiographical novel, also titled *The Human Revolution*:

> As Mr. Gan read the "Virtuous Practices" chapter of the
> Sutra of Immeasurable Meanings and reached the verse

[containing the thirty-four negations], there, in the deep recesses of the thick spectacles he wore, a brilliant white light flashed in his eyes. It was no longer his eyes that were moving down the page. Neither was he reading the sutra with his intellect: He was pounding his still robust body against each word and phrase of the verse.

Ikeda: He was truly trying to read the sutra with his whole being. The Lotus Sutra teaches that all people can attain Buddhahood. What, then, is a Buddha? What does it mean to attain Buddhahood? These questions are vital to all Buddhist teachings. Mr. Toda deeply contemplated these questions and sought to resolve them. It was then that the word *life* suddenly flashed in his mind. He finally perceived that the Buddha is life itself:

> *Life is neither existing nor not existing,*
> *neither caused nor conditioned, neither self nor other,*
> *neither square nor round, neither short nor long,...*
> *neither crimson nor purple nor any other sort of color.*

Endo: His thoughts raced with excitement: "The Buddha is life itself! It is an expression of life! The Buddha does not exist outside ourselves but within our lives. No, it exists outside our lives as well. It is the real entity of the cosmic life!"

Saito: Mr. Toda used the word *life* precisely because he had perceived the Buddha as a real entity.

Ikeda: Yes. *Life* is a straightforward, familiar word we use every day. But at the same time it can express the most profound essence of the Buddhist Law, a single word that expresses infinite meaning. All humans are endowed with life, so this word has practical, concrete meaning for everyone. In this way, Mr. Toda's realization made Buddhism comprehensible to all.

Life has enormous diversity. It is rich and filled with energy. At the same time, it operates according to certain laws and has a definite rhythm. The doctrine of 'three thousand realms in a single moment of life' describes this harmony of diversity, and one who has perceived the essence of this principle is a Buddha.

Life is also free and unfettered. It is an open entity in constant communication with the external world, always exchanging matter and energy and information. Yet while open, it maintains its autonomy. Life is characterized by this harmonious freedom and an openness to the entire universe.

The infinite and unbounded state of Buddhahood can be described as a state in which the freedom, openness and harmony of life are maximally realized. Nichiren Daishonin says *myo* [of *myoho*, the Mystic Law] has three meanings: "to open," "to be endowed and perfect" and "to revive." These are the attributes of life and the attributes of a Buddha as well. In one sense, we can regard all Buddhist scriptures as presenting a philosophy of life.

T'ien-t'ai Buddhism represents the teaching that the Great Teacher "T'ien-t'ai himself practiced in the depths of his own being."[2] Furthermore, the Daishonin declares, "The eighty-four thousand teachings [all the innumerable teachings Shakyamuni preached during his lifetime] are the diary of one's own being (GZ, 563).

I still remember how Mr. Toda once chuckled and said that he could physically perceive and share "the teaching that the Great Teacher T'ien-t'ai himself practiced in the depths of his own being."

He said to me: "Dai, you have to encounter problems in life. Only when we encounter problems can we understand faith and achieve greatness." I was twenty-seven at the time, fighting illness, and Mr. Toda was trying to encourage me in this way to bring forth greater life force. I was very moved by his words, and I noted them in my diary. Actually, at the time, Mr. Toda himself was in extremely poor health, his body gaunt and wasted. Despite that, he was always thinking about how to encourage young people, how to enable them to attain the same state of life as he.

Saito: This attests to Mr. Toda's sublime state of life and the noble bonds that exist between mentor and disciple.

Ikeda: Mr. Toda once described his feelings after having attained his realization in prison as follows: "It is like lying on your back in a wide open space looking up at the sky with arms and legs outstretched. All that you wish for immediately appears. No matter how much you may give away, there is always more. It is never exhausted. Try and see if you can attain this state of life. If you really want to, then I suggest you spend a little time in prison for the sake of the Lotus Sutra, for the sake of propagating Nichiren Daishonin's Buddhism!"

He also said, however: "The times are different now, so you don't need to spend time in prison. Still, you must fight with every ounce of your strength to spread the Daishonin's Buddhism."

Suda: Mr. Toda's realization was not simply intellectual; it signified a transformation of his life itself.

Ikeda: Yes, that's true. The purpose of Buddhism, ultimately, is to transform one's inner state of life.

The Soka Gakkai was not the first to speak of Buddhism as a philosophy of life. The Daishonin's Buddhism is by its very nature a philosophy of life, and the Soka Gakkai is heir to that Buddhism.

Shakyamuni confronted the sufferings of human life — birth, aging, sickness and death — and, in struggling to understand them, he opened a vast world in the innermost depths of his being. Later, basing himself on the Lotus Sutra, T'ien-t'ai observed the inner reality of his own life and expressed what he realized in the form of the principle of three thousand realms in a single moment of life.

T'ien-t'ai also used a concept expounded in the Flower Garland Sutra — that there are no distinctions among the mind, the Buddha and human beings — to discuss the Mystic Law revealed in the Lotus Sutra. *Life* is also a familiar contemporary word that can give unified expression to all three of these dimensions.

Nichiren Daishonin, meanwhile, realized that Nam-myoho-renge-kyo is the true entity of life. He inscribed the Gohonzon, the object of devotion, and expounded his philosophy in the "Record of the Orally Transmitted Teachings" and other writings so that all could realize the true entity of life and open the path to happiness.

In other words, throughout its history, Buddhism has fundamentally always been a philosophy of life.

Saito: The question then is how to enable others to realize this vital point. This has posed a rigorous challenge to Buddhist philosophers and scholars through the ages.

Ikeda: Yes. Mr. Toda's "The Philosophy of Life" was not merely an expression of intellectual theory. Nor did he arrive at it through repeated scientific or rational steps of analysis and synthesis. Yet, at the same time, it is not inconsistent with science or reason. Mr. Toda drew forth his philosophy of life from the depths of the Lotus Sutra in his own desperate all-out struggle for the ultimate truth —a struggle that engaged his entire being. Indeed, his philosophy represents the wisdom of the Lotus Sutra.

His philosophy, therefore, not only informs us of the nature of life but has the power to transform our way of thinking. It leads to hope and practical action. It is a philosophy of practical relevance—an "actual" philosophy that brings forth a powerful energy for living. When we faithfully translate this philosophy into practice, our personal drama of self-reformation—in which we change a life of powerlessness and despair into one of satisfaction and happiness—begins.

That reformation of the individual spurs reformation on every level. It is the first turn of the wheel in the process to make humanity strong, rich and wise.

Saito: You are speaking of 'human revolution' and of 'all-embracing revolution.'

Ikeda: Human revolution is a contemporary expression for the attainment of Buddhahood for the individual, while an all-embracing revolution refers to kosen-rufu.

The relationship between the two resembles that of the rotation and revolution of the Earth, which, while rotating on its own axis, simultaneously orbits the sun. The Earth's rotation on its axis produces day and night, while its movement around the sun produces the four seasons.

Bathed in the light of the Buddhist Law, we also experience night and day in the course of creating our own history of human revolution toward limitless improvement. We experience winter and spring as we continue to play out the exciting drama of kosen-rufu through the changing seasons. The Soka Gakkai begins and ends with the philosophy set forth by Mr. Toda; its essence lies in his realization that the Buddha is life itself.

Moreover, as Mr. Toda continued in prison to probe the essence of the Lotus Sutra, he saw himself attending the Ceremony in the Air as a Bodhisattva of the Earth. However, I will leave a discussion of the significance of this experience for another chapter.

Endo: In the past the priests of Nichiren Shoshu criticized the lay members' use of the word *enlightenment* for Mr. Toda's experience. It seems they were not at all pleased by the prospect of mere lay people becoming enlightened.

Saito: Saying that those who devote themselves to Buddhism are not allowed to attain enlightenment is like saying that those in college are not allowed to graduate. In the end, such warped thinking is purely the product of jealousy.

Suda: In the phrase "The Buddha is life itself," *life* has a scientific yet warm ring to it.

Ikeda: Yes, and we can see Mr. Toda's greatness in making that identification. With the word *Buddha*, the image of a supreme being tends to dominate people's impression; it evokes a feeling of the Buddha being somehow distant and separate from them. The word *law*, in the sense that it implies a rule or phenomenon, suggests the impersonal. Alone, it does not convey much warmth. Essentially, the Buddha and the Law are not two separate things—the word *life* encompasses both.

All people are endowed with life, and life is immeasurably precious. No one can deny this. The declaration that "The Buddha is life itself" reveals that the very essence of Buddhism exists in our own lives.

Saito: I agree completely. Nonetheless, I can't help feeling that all too often we still only understand the word *life* intellectually— especially in such expressions as "life throughout the past, present and future" or "eternal life." How should we comprehend life?

Ikeda: Mr. Toda often said, "Though we speak of 'life throughout the past, present and future,' or 'eternal life,' it is something that no one has ever seen." Still, I think it's worthwhile to try to sketch an outline of the concept of eternal life as a point of reference.

Suda: Here's one perspective. In each of us there is something called a "self." That self continues even after we die. That self is the real essence of life.

Ikeda: I see. Where is that self after one dies?

Suda: Let me see…. Well, I don't think of it as something ethereal, like the image of a ghost, anyway.

Ikeda: Mr. Toda had something to say on this matter: "We use the word *self* [to refer to ourselves], but this word actually refers to the universe. When we ask how the life of the universe is different from the life of each one of you, the only differences are those of your bodies and minds. Your [individual] life and that of the universe are the same."

We tend to think of the universe and human beings as separate entities, but Mr. Toda declares that they are identical in that both are life.

Suda: Mr. Toda's philosophy of life states that the universe is life itself, and that life, together with the universe, has always existed and will continue eternally. He said, "Just as we sleep and wake and then sleep again, we live and die and then live again, maintaining life eternally." He also said: "When we wake up in the morning, we resume our activities based on the same mind as the previous day. In the same way, in each new existence we are destined to live based on the result of the karmic causes created in our previous lives."

Endo: Let us suppose there is a tall tree, and that we call this tall tree the universe. Countless leaves and flowers grow on it. Could we perhaps regard individual lives as represented by the leaves and flowers of this tree?

Ikeda: Someone once asked President Toda a similar question. He answered:

> I don't think it's correct to say that our lives grow forth from something [like buds or shoots on a tree]. Let's suppose the water in this teacup in front of me is the universe. When the wind blows, it creates ripples on the water's surface. Those ripples are our lives. They also represent one of the workings of the life of the universe. Therefore, if the wind disappears, the ripples, too, will disappear, and the water will return to its original state.

In other words, he says, when we liken the universe to the ocean, our lives are like the waves that appear and disappear on the surface of the ocean of the universe.

Endo: The waves and the ocean are not separate entities. According to Mr. Toda, the waves are but part of the ongoing activity of the ocean.

Saito: That reminds me of a remark by the British philosopher Alan Watts: "There is no separate 'you' to get something out of the universe.... As the ocean 'waves' so the universe 'peoples'.... What we therefore see as 'death,' empty space or nothingness is only the trough between the crests of this endless waving ocean of life."[3]

Suda: I guess this means that our lives are fused with the universe.

Ikeda: Yes, that may be one way to describe it. But Mr. Toda said: "Rather than 'fused' with the universe, we *are* the life of the universe itself. And that life itself causes changes."

Endo: Some say our lives are like a flowing river. The river flows continuously, always changing, until it finally merges with the ocean.

Ikeda: I see. But don't our lives have a deeper dimension? Mr. Toda described them as the very basis of all things, which we perceive as changing and flowing. But, actually, the true nature of life is neither flowing nor still; it is like empty space, he said.

It is a reality that is at once the infinite macrocosm and the microcosms that are each of the countless individual living beings. It is an enormous life-entity, always undergoing dynamic change while at the same time being eternal and everlasting. The Buddha and the Mystic Law are names we give this undeniable entity of cosmic life. We are all embodiments of this sublime entity.

The Lotus Sutra teaches "the true entity of all phenomena" (LS2, 24). "All phenomena" refers to each individual living thing. The "true entity" of this phenomena is cosmic life itself. Mr. Toda expressed this ineffable truth as "the Buddha is life itself." Once we understand this, it is inconceivable to think of killing others, because to destroy someone else is only to destroy ourselves.

Saito: American author and educator Helen Keller, who as a young child lost her sight and hearing and was unable to speak, once wrote: "Here in the midst of everyday air, I sense the rush of ethereal rains. I am conscious of the splendor that binds all things of the earth to all things of heaven."[4] I can't help thinking that Helen Keller, despite her blindness and deafness, clearly "saw" the interrelationship of the macrocosm and the microcosm.

Ikeda: Buddhism teaches five types of vision: the 'physical eye of ordinary mortals,' the 'divine eye,' the 'eye of wisdom,' the 'eye of the Law' and the 'eye of the Buddha.' Helen Keller may have looked at the world through her life itself—an eye far sharper and more perceptive than ordinary physical vision. Or, to put it another way, perhaps life truly can be "seen" only when one probes into it on the profoundest level.

Suda: Modern science may be regarded as an eye of wisdom of sorts, but the tendency of science has been to look at life as a kind of machine made up of various parts. Science has also sought to gain insights into life and human beings by dividing them into opposing elements such as body and spirit, self and other. It has tried to grasp the workings of life by reducing them all to material things.

But though an aspect of life may be explained by such mechanistic theories, by dualism and reductionism, it does not give us a picture of life in its dynamic entirety.

Saito: Science has in fact encouraged a materialistic view of human beings and life, a perspective in which adversarial relationships dominate not only among living things but between living things and their environment. This has in turn led people to destroy the environment and to exploit the natural world.

Endo: Much soul-searching on this destructive course of humanity gave rise to new sciences and greater ecological awareness in the 1980s. Fritjof Capra's *The Tao of Physics*[5] urges a transcendence of dualism and reductionism and outlines truths common to the cutting edge of physics and the wisdom of Eastern thought. Lyall Watson's *Lifetide*[6] presents the idea that living things on Earth are not discrete entities but live in symbiosis, in a matrix of interrelations. Jim E. Lovelock's *Gaia—A New Look at Life on Earth*[7] explores the Gaia hypothesis that the Earth itself is one giant living organism.

Gradually, forgotten values such as harmony with nature, a sense of unity with others, equality and diversity are being rediscovered and emphasized by thinkers such as these.

Ikeda: Science is beginning to look seriously at the interdependence of all things, what is described in Buddhism as 'dependent origination.'

Saito: The unified view of nature, of life phenomena, held by German poet Johann Wolfgang von Goethe is also being rediscovered. Goethe writes:

> The time will inevitably come when mechanistic and atomic thinking will be put out of the minds of all people of wisdom, and instead dynamics and chemistry will come to be seen in all phenomena. When that happens, the divinity of living Nature will unfold before our eyes all the more clearly.[8]

Suda: Some people urge us to change from a material view of the world to a phenomenal view.

Ikeda: Phenomena are the Law itself. People are coming to see the world as not made up of things but of phenomena. The Lotus Sutra, as I have mentioned, teaches the true entity of all phenomena.

As your comments indicate, clearly we are moving toward a major paradigm shift in our views of life and the world. This view of the world as a living entity approaches, from one perspective, Mr. Toda's realization.

Endo: Even fields of the most materialistic branches of science are being forced to consider a phenomenal view of the world and of life. Quantum mechanics is an example that comes to mind. Some physicists are still trying to find conclusive evidence of the existence of ultimate particles, but they are finding that elementary particles can be defined only in terms of the conditions under which they are observed.

DNA (deoxyribonucleic acid) research in molecular biology is another good example. Up to now, scientists have attempted to take the DNA molecule apart and separately consider the function of each piece of its genetic information. This is an attempt to understand DNA mechanistically—in terms of its material composition.

Although the basic method of study perhaps remains the same, scientists recently have been working to shed light on the function of entire DNA molecules specific to a particular species [for example, human genomic DNA], and to decipher from them the story of life on earth. Scientists speculate this will enable them to investigate the history of the interaction among living things and also the responses of life to its environment since life appeared on this planet. Some, incidentally, have even likened DNA to the Buddhist scriptures or to the Bible.

Therefore, while science still remains rooted in the material, we are beginning to see a shift toward the phenomenal, toward life

—a shift from viewing things as static objects to viewing things as having a living story to tell.

Ikeda: The times are changing rapidly. One important point to remember about DNA is that life created DNA and not the other way round. The universe is identical to life, and life is identical to the universe. Life itself is the creator, and it is the created as well.

Suda: Speaking of creation, we also see new trends in art. In addition to the inorganic, geometric beauty that has characterized much of modern art, we are beginning to see a more living type of artistic beauty, a revival of life force in art.

For example, in "simulated life art," the organic beauty of such things as cells are reproduced by computer. And "healing art" employs certain forms and colors in an effort to comfort and soothe those who are sick and enhance their natural recuperative powers.

Endo: In business, too, we see signs of a trend away from the simple production of goods to a restoration of life, a restoration of humane values.

Suda: We also see new efforts to move away from power politics to nonviolence and nonkilling, that is, from government based on military strength to that based on reverence for life. The 1986 "people power" revolution in the Philippines, the 1989 restoration of democracy to Chile and the "Velvet Revolution" in Czechoslovakia were all achieved without violence. Many problems remain to be solved in each of these nations, but I think they now have hopes of establishing a foundation of respect for human life.

Ikeda: I believe that *life* and *life force* will be the keywords for the twenty-first century. In a recent address,[9] Václav Havel, president of the Czech Republic (and formerly of Czechoslovakia), asked what was necessary for democracy today to revitalize humanity.

He suggested that the democratic societies were afflicted with materialism and "the denial of any kind of spirituality. They showed "a proud disdain for everything supra-personal," "a frenzied consumerism" and "an absence of faith in a higher order of things or simply in eternity."

"Were I to compare democracy to life-giving radiation, I would say that while from the political point of view it is the only hope for humanity, it can only have a beneficial impact on us if it resonates with our deepest inner nature."[10]

In the sense that it is "life-giving radiation," he said, it is vital that democracy spread across the world. But democracy as we see it today has also forgotten something. "Wherein lies that forgotten dimension of democracy that could give it universal resonance?" President Havel asked and then presented his conclusion:

> If democracy is not only to survive but to expand successfully and resolve those conflicts of cultures, then, in my opinion, it must rediscover and renew its own transcendental origins. It must renew its respect for that nonmaterial order which is not only above us but also in us and among us, and which is the only possible and reliable source of man's respect for himself, for others.... The authority of a world democratic order simply cannot be built on anything else but the revitalized authority of the universe.[11]

From a Buddhist perspective, a "nonmaterial order" can be described as an order of life. Mr. Havel says we must revive reverence for that order and restore the "authority of the universe." As he has indicated, people around the world now search for a free yet not intemperate form of society, a society rich in spirituality. At the same time, they seek a sound view of life, a reviving wisdom that will serve as the foundation of that society. Political leaders around the world must now pursue such wisdom.

Saito: Speaking of the relationship between democracy and a sound view of life, Dr. Alexander S. Tsipko, director of the Moscow-based International Foundation for Socioeconomic and Political Studies (the Gorbachev Foundation), contributed these remarks to a Japanese newspaper:

> Now we see the complete collapse of the Soviet Union
> .... The war in Chechen has not only been a defeat for
> Russia's young democracy: it represents the utter moral
> collapse of Russia.... It is unlikely that the Russian Fed-
> eration, isolated and its future unpredictable, will be rec-
> ognized or viewed favorably by the world. What the
> world has gained instead of a new democratic Russia is
> a nation that values human life very little and that seeks
> to solve its domestic problems with tanks and guns, a
> nation whose government is incapable of exercising con-
> trol over anyone or anything. It is difficult to imagine a
> way out of this dead end that Russia has put itself in. Is
> there, in fact, a way out?[12]

Endo: Many precious lives were lost in that war. I've also heard reports that many of the soldiers were little more than boys. Some mothers were so worried about their sons in the army that they journeyed to the battlefront to check on their safety.

Ikeda: No matter how people may try to justify war, there are no just wars in this world. None at all. Those who suffer in war are always ordinary people, families, mothers. I lost my eldest brother, Kiichi, in World War II. He died fighting in Burma (now Myanmar) on January 11, 1945. He was only twenty-nine. It took more than two years for the news of his death to reach my family.

In the period just after the war ended, my mother said to me joyously on several occasions: "I had a dream about Kiichi. He told me, 'Don't worry, I'm fine. I'm coming back alive,' and then left." Her brave optimistic words and actions only made our hearts ache for her all the more. I remember her deep grief when she received the report of Kiichi's death, and her last thread of hope was cut. And I remember her clutching the urn containing his ashes to her bosom when they were returned to us. Those scenes are forever branded in my memory.

Dr. Tsipko used the expression "a nation that values human life very little." The real question is whether we look at human life from the point of view of the nation or of life. The eyes of the nation are quick to use human life as a slave to the interests of those in power, reducing people to numbers and objects. But the eyes of life view each individual as a precious, irreplaceable and unique existence.

Mr. Toda's enlightenment that the Buddha is life itself is a declaration that life is the absolute and supreme reality. It was his initial challenge to all warped and twisted points of view that would destroy the dignity of human life. Indeed this is Buddhism's fundamental challenge.

Endo: The defeat of Russia's young democracy of which Dr. Tsipko speaks is also a tragedy arising from what Mr. Havel describes as "a lack of reverence for a nonmaterial order" or, in other words, a lack of reverence for life.

Suda: Reverence for life was also the final theme of President Ikeda's dialogue with Dr. Arnold Toynbee. I sensed there a remarkable commitment bidding farewell to an age in which ideology took priority over life, a commitment to make the twenty-first century a century of life.

Ikeda: Yes, and it was Mr. Toda who first opened the door to that century of life. Embracing his spirit with my own life, I have traveled around the world stressing respect for the dignity of human life. Mr. Toda's philosophy was incredibly insightful, the crystallization of a great truth, as history will demonstrate without a doubt.

NOTES

1. The thirty-four negations describing the entity of the Buddha appear in "Virtuous Practices," the first chapter of the Sutra of Immeasurable Meanings. The entire passage reads:

   His body neither existing nor not existing,
   neither caused nor conditioned, neither self nor other,
   neither square nor round, neither short nor long,
   neither appearing nor disappearing, neither born nor extinguished,
   neither created nor arising, neither acted nor made,
   neither sitting nor lying down, neither walking nor standing,
   neither moving nor turning, neither idle nor still,
   neither advancing nor retreating, neither in safety nor in danger,
   neither right nor wrong, neither gaining nor losing,
   neither that nor this, neither departing nor coming,
   neither blue nor yellow, neither red nor white,
   neither crimson nor purple nor any other sort of color.

2. Chang-an, direct disciple and legitimate successor of the Great Teacher T'ien-t'ai, states, "*Great Concentration and Insight* [by T'ien-t'ai] reveals the teaching that T'ien-t'ai Chih-che himself practiced in the depths of his being" (WND, p. 355).

3. Quoted in: Guy Murchie, *The Seven Mysteries of Life* (Boston: Houghton Mifflin Company, 1978), p. 53.

4. Quoted in Murchie, ibid.

5. Fritjof Capra, *The Tao of Physics: An Exploration of the Parallels Between Modern Physics and Eastern Mysticism* (Boston: Shambhala Publications, Inc., 1991).

6. Lyall Watson, *Lifetide—The Biology of the Unconscious* (New York: Simon and Schuster, 1979).

7. Jim E. Lovelock, *Gaia—A New Look at Life on Earth* (London: Oxford University Press, 1987).

8. Translated from Japanese: From Goethe's diary (1812). Ludwig von Bertaannffy, *Seimei* (Life), trans. Kei Nagano and Mamoru Iijima (Tokyo: Miscuzu Shobo, 1974), p. 59.

9. "Civilization as a Contemporary Political Condition," delivered at Stanford University, September 29, 1994.

10. Ibid.

11. Ibid.

12. *Hokkaido Shimbun* (The Hokkaido Times), January 6, 1995.

3 A Scripture That Calls Out
to All People

Ikeda: Many people in the world still know nothing of Nichiren Daishonin's Buddhism, or, if they have heard of it, seriously misunderstand it. Therefore, let us leave behind a record of our conversations for future generations—a record of which we can be proud.

Suda: In Japan, the Daishonin's teachings, which were often exploited by militarist authorities, have been branded as ultranationalistic, but, in fact, nothing could be further from the truth.

Ikeda: Yes. That is another reason for our discussion of the Lotus Sutra—to find the best way to communicate Nichiren Daishonin's Buddhism correctly to people around the world.

The Daishonin expounded the very essence of the Lotus Sutra, so studying it is the same as studying the Daishonin's teachings. By the same token, studying the Daishonin's teachings leads to an understanding of the Lotus Sutra. They are like two sides of the same coin. Consequently, when we discuss the Lotus Sutra, we are not simply studying the teachings of Shakyamuni. Looking toward the distant future, we are undertaking the far more challenging task of exploring Nichiren Daishonin's teachings.

The teachings of Buddhism are profound, and it is often said that words cannot do them justice. Nevertheless, words are our only means of communicating them. I hope our discussion serves as an opportunity to introduce others to a proper understanding of the Daishonin's teachings and that it will advance our efforts for worldwide propagation of his Buddhism and bring hope to people across the globe. This kind of dialogue, in a sense, is something we must work at throughout our entire lives.

Endo: What really impresses me about the reader responses [to the serialized version of these discussions] is the strong seeking spirit shown by members of the women's and young women's divisions. Their eagerness to learn and their desire for self-improvement are really wonderful.

Ikeda: That's absolutely true. In fact, our men's and young men's division members are no match for them! The women of the SGI are pure-hearted and dedicated. Women are said to place more importance on grasping the reality and substance of a thing than being satisfied with a merely conceptual understanding.

The benefits enjoyed by those who study Buddhism earnestly and share the teachings with others are enormous. They are certain to attain the level of great Buddhist scholars such as Shariputra in lifetime after lifetime.

Suda: I'd like to share with you a story cited by Dr. Hajime Nakamura, the renowned Japanese Buddhologist, about the active role played by female followers of Buddhism in ancient times:

About one or two hundred years after Buddhism emerged, a Greek ambassador of the king of Syria visited India and was astonished at what he observed there. A surprising thing about India, he exclaimed, is that there are women philosophers who debate openly with men, propounding the most difficult arguments!

Dr. Nakamura continues: "The appearance of an order of [Buddhist] nuns was an astonishing development in world religious history. No such female religious order existed in Europe, North Africa, West Asia, or East Asia at that time. Buddhism was the first religion to produce one."[1]

Ikeda: That women possess a solid command of philosophy, which they can articulate with confidence and eloquence, is a matter of common knowledge in today's SGI, but back in those days, it was extremely rare for women to do so.

Saito: The status of women in ancient India was said to be nearly as low as that of slaves. Shakyamuni's inclusion of women in the religious order he founded was a revolutionary act.

Endo: Calls for greater opportunities for women to become leaders in a variety of fields are now being heard in the religious world. For example, the Church of England recently ordained its first female priest, while a movement is under way to improve the status of nuns in the Roman Catholic Church.

Ikeda: The teachings of Buddhism were expounded for the happiness of all people; there is no discrimination based on sex, priestly or lay status, race, academic achievement, social position, power or wealth. In fact, Buddhism was expounded precisely to enable the discriminated and oppressed, those who have experienced the bitterest sufferings, to attain supreme happiness. This is the true power of Buddhism and the true wisdom of the Lotus Sutra.

Endo: Speaking of equality for women, the scriptures of Mahayana Buddhism, including the Lotus Sutra, make frequent use of the form of address "good men and good women." This originally referred to men and women of good families and came to indicate men and women of the laity. The inclusion of "good women" on an equal footing with "good men" in this expression indicates the many active women followers in the orders of Mahayana Buddhism.

Ikeda: That seems reasonable, especially when we look at our present SGI women's division. Returning to the expression "good men and good women," I think it is used in the Lotus Sutra not to make a distinction between lay practitioners and priests but instead to transcend that division. I believe these men and women are referred to as "good" not because they come from good families but because they have made the commitment to follow the path to Buddhahood set forth by Shakyamuni—in other words, the path to true independence as human beings and victory in life. "Good" here refers not to lineage but to goodness of intent.

Saito: I agree. In particular, in the sutra sections where Shakyamuni encourages upholding and propagating the scriptures after his death, he constantly addresses his listeners, "good men and good women." Unless they are truly committed people, whether lay practitioners or priests, they cannot carry out the difficult tasks of upholding and propagating the Lotus Sutra after Shakyamuni's passing.

Ikeda: The Lotus Sutra is a scripture open to the people. It has remained alive over the centuries precisely because those who embraced and propagated it went amongst the people to expound its teachings.

Saito: Our theme today is the question: For whom was the Lotus Sutra expounded? I hope that through our discussion we can make it vividly clear that it is a scripture for the people.

Ikeda: This is a very important theme in trying to understand the true essence of the Lotus Sutra. Nichiren Daishonin discusses this issue in such writings as "The Object of Devotion for Observing the Mind" and "The Essence of the Lotus Sutra."

Endo: In the Lotus Sutra, Shakyamuni expounds his teachings to different listeners. For example, in "Expedient Means"—the main chapter of the first half, that is, the theoretical teachings—he speaks to Shariputra, a voice-hearer (Skt *shravaka*; a person of learning). While in "Life Span"—the central chapter of the second half, that is, the essential teachings—Shakyamuni directs his discourse to Bodhisattva Maitreya. The important question is, to whom are these teachings of the Lotus Sutra directed as a whole?

Suda: In "The Essence of the Lotus Sutra," Nichiren Daishonin says that both the essential and theoretical teachings were for all people living after Shakyamuni's passing; the sutra, he concludes, was taught particularly for people of the Latter Day of the Law. Moreover, he says it was specifically expounded for "Nichiren himself" (GZ, 331–38).

Ikeda: In that assertion—that the sutra was taught for the sake of those living after Shakyamuni's passing, for the people of the Latter Day of the Law—the compassion of the Lotus Sutra, which extends to all people, is apparent.

The Lotus Sutra teaches that the "one great reason" why Buddhas appear in the world—in other words, the supreme and ultimate purpose for the advent of Buddhas—is to enable all living beings to attain Buddhahood (LS2, 31).

This goal cannot be accomplished unless the teachings preached by Shakyamuni are also effective for all those living after him, particularly those in the defiled age of the Latter Day of the Law. It is inconceivable, therefore, that the Buddha would fail to leave behind teachings for those living in later ages. The Lotus Sutra is the compassionate scripture he taught for precisely that reason.

Nichiren Daishonin read the Lotus Sutra with his life, revealing and propagating Nam-myoho-renge-kyo as the Law implicit in this sutra, which is designed to enable all people to become happy. The Daishonin was the first to demonstrate how to realize the ideal of the Lotus Sutra to bring happiness to all people in the Latter Day of the Law, when the Buddha's teachings were predicted to perish. Based on this awareness and conviction, the Daishonin could then declare that, of all the people in the Latter Day, the Lotus Sutra had been taught specifically for him. In that sense, it is possible for us to regard the Lotus Sutra as predicting the Daishonin's appearance.

Suda: Only a heartless Buddha would fail to care about the fate of those living after him and refuse to teach them the path to happiness. The "Life Span" chapter speaks conclusively about the salvation of those who live after Shakyamuni's passing. This is evident in the famous parable of the excellent physician and his sick children, expounded in this chapter.

Endo: The parable tells of a father who is an excellent physician. While he is away, his children drink poison, and he returns home to find them writhing on the ground in agony. The physician prepares medicine for his children, but they refuse to take it, for the poison has caused them to lose their minds.

The father then devises a plan to save his children. Leaving behind the medicine, he sets off on a journey. Reaching his destination, he sends a messenger to tell his children that he has died. They are so overcome with grief that they regain their senses, drink the medicine and are immediately cured.

The excellent physician is the Buddha, and the journey on which he departs represents the Buddha's passing. Nichiren Daishonin further says that the children indicate the people living in the Latter Day of the Law, the good medicine is Nam-myoho-renge-kyo, and the messenger refers to the Bodhisattvas of the Earth. In other words, Nam-myoho-renge-kyo, the excellent medicine that saves all people after the Buddha's passing, has been expounded in the "Life Span" chapter.

Ikeda: A Buddha is a person awakened to the reality of his or her being and, naturally, to the reality of all human life. That is the wisdom of the Buddha and the wisdom of the Lotus Sutra.

The Lotus Sutra was clearly expounded for all human beings, to enable them to attain true independence. It does not discriminate in any sense between priests and lay practitioners, men and women, rich and poor, persons of high and low status, or young and old. It is entirely for all humanity.

Saito: In the sutra known as his "declaration of propagation," Shakyamuni states that he transmits the Law "for the happiness, benefit and peace of the people."[2] In Sanskrit texts of the Lotus Sutra, precisely the same words appear several times where the "one great reason" for Buddhas appearing in this world is explained. In the Chinese translation by Kumarajiva[3], who preferred brevity, these phrases are condensed into a single instance: to "benefit and bring peace and happiness to living beings in large measure" (LS2, 32). This passage tells us that the Lotus Sutra was expounded for the true happiness and peace of all people.

Ikeda: Nichiren Daishonin writes: "If you chant Nam-myoho-renge-kyo with your whole heart, you will naturally become endowed with the Buddha's thirty-two features and eighty characteristics.[4] As the sutra says, 'hoping to make all persons equal to me, without any distinction between us'" (WND, 1030).

The Lotus Sutra teaches that all equally possess the potential for Buddhahood and that all have the ability to savor a state of absolute happiness. It is worth noting that Shakyamuni's intent to make Buddhahood accessible to all people is revealed by the language he chose to preach the Buddhist teachings: the language of Magadha,[5] the everyday language of the common people.

Endo: Yes. Orthodox Brahmanism of the time insisted that the holy teachings could only be transmitted in the sacred language of the Vedas, a language used only by the upper, educated class. From ancient times, it had been forbidden to address people of lower castes or those outside the caste system, the untouchables, in this language.

Suda: On one occasion, two of Shakyamuni's followers said to him: "By preaching the honorable and excellent teachings in the vernacular of the people, you harm the dignity of Buddhism. From now on, please preach in the noble and elevated language of the Vedas." These followers were brothers, educated members of the

Brahman caste, who had been so moved by Shakyamuni's preaching that they had joined the order. "Never!" declared the Buddha in response to their request, putting an end to the matter. It is even said that he prescribed punishment for anyone who dared preach Buddhism in the language of the Vedas.

Ikeda: That episode clearly demonstrates Shakyamuni's powerful desire to make Buddhism available to all, regardless of social class.

The Daishonin also wrote many of his letters to his lay practitioners in the Japanese phonetic script known as *hiragana,* so that they could read them easily. [In other words, he used the language of the common people instead of the scholarly classical Chinese script used in formal writings in those days.] It is well known that after his death, a number of high-ranking priests among his followers regarded these *hiragana* writings as an embarrassment and burned them or had the paper on which they were written reprocessed into fresh paper, obliterating the Daishonin's writings.

Endo: You are speaking of the five disloyal senior priests. All of them were very close disciples of the Daishonin, yet this incident shows how little they understood his heart. Nikko Shonin, the Daishonin's successor and the second high priest, discusses this in his "Guidelines for the Believers of the Fuji School" (GZ, 1604). He also states that at the time of the widespread propagation of the Daishonin's Buddhism, his writings should be translated into all the languages of the world (GZ, 1613).

Ikeda: The SGI is ensuring that Nikko Shonin's wish becomes a reality.

It is no outstanding distinction to simply know what your teacher has taught; what matters most is the reason or purpose for which you know those teachings. Anyone can say, "My mentor's teachings are wonderful!" But Nikko Shonin took the next step: "Since they're so wonderful, I must share them with others no matter what!" The five senior priests, on the other hand, thought themselves great simply because they knew of these magnificent teachings.

At first glance, it may appear that they all revere and respect their mentor, but the difference between the two types of disciples is as vast as that between heaven and earth, fire and water. It is important not to be mistaken on this point.

Mahayana Buddhism does not subscribe to a complicated list of rules of behavior or discipline with which to bind people. It respects the freedom and autonomy of the individual. However, when we hold the teachings of Mahayana Buddhism up before the mirror of the people, they offer an extremely demanding model of leadership. This is because irresponsibility is not permitted.

Suda: The Lotus Sutra — the pinnacle of Mahayana Buddhism — harshly criticizes corrupt and degenerate religious leaders and priests. There is a famous verse portion in the "Encouraging Devotion" chapter, which speaks of the three powerful enemies of Buddhism, describing priests who pretend to have attained enlightenment but are in fact in earnest pursuit of their own greedy desires (LS13, 193–95).

Endo: There is also a well-known stone inscription of an edict by India's King Ashoka, who lived about a century after Shakyamuni's death, which says, "Drive corrupt priests from the Buddhist order!"

Ikeda: A sad but true fact we must solemnly recognize is that the corruption of priests began soon after Shakyamuni's death. Religion is always in danger of growing apart from the people when its leaders forget to reflect carefully on their own behavior and come to look upon themselves as authorities.

Suda: Like Buddhism as a whole, the Lotus Sutra was also taught in the language of the people. Many Sanskrit versions of the Lotus Sutra exist today, and each of them is written in a style that incorporates vernacular elements of the different regions from which they originate. Buddhist scriptures, of course, did not begin as written texts; they were transmitted orally. As they were transmitted from person to person, over many years and through many countries, expressions unique to each region, time and people were incorporated into the scripture, and in the process many transcriptions, each with a distinct personality, were produced.

Endo: The expression "teacher of the Law" is another example of the people-oriented nature of the sutra. In the Lotus Sutra, a teacher of the Law is someone who propagates the Lotus Sutra after Shakyamuni's death. The Japanese word *hosshi* is usually thought to refer to a priest. Its original meaning, however, is simply "one who teaches the Law," and it includes both priests and lay practitioners. In the Lotus Sutra, Shakyamuni addresses these teachers of the Law as "good men and good women" (LS10, 161).

Suda: In fact, if we look at the origins of "teacher of the Law," it was more likely to refer to a lay person than a priest. The Sanskrit rendering of this term is *dharma-bhanaka*: *Dharma* means "law" and *bhanaka* means "one who memorizes and recites the scriptures." In some scriptures [such as the Daiji (Skt Mahavastu) Sutra, a writing on the Buddha's advent and life], the *bhanaka* is described as a type of musical performer, including dancers and players of musical instruments. In the monastic tradition of Theravada Buddhism of those days, practitioners were forbidden to attend musical or theatrical performances, so the *bhanaka* are believed to have been lay persons not associated with Theravada Buddhism.

Saito: Many people tend to accept the premise that Buddhism distinguishes between priests and lay practitioners. In Japan, in particular, there is a strong preconception that Buddhism is a religion carried out by professional priests, where the laity make offerings to the priests and, in exchange, the priests pray for the laity.

The distinction between priests and laity, however, really reflects only the cultural situation in Indian society when Buddhism originated. It clearly has no basis in Buddhist teachings. The Buddhologist Kyosei Hayashima notes: "As far as the formation of the *samgha* (Buddhist order) is concerned, the division of the Buddha's followers into priests and laity, both of which aimed for an identical ultimate goal, was no more than a reflection of the social structure of the time in which the Buddha lived."[6]

Endo: Nichiko, the fifty-ninth high priest of Nichiren Shoshu, remarked, "The distinction between priests and laity has always been a social convention, but it cannot be regarded as necessarily appropriate."[7] In other words, depending upon the age and the society, it may not be appropriate to distinguish between priests and laity.

Suda: There may have been some meaning in distinguishing between priests and laity when the laity had no detailed knowledge of religion and was forced to rely on priests as religious specialists, as it were. But today information and education are available to all members of society, and priests can no longer claim exclusive knowledge or authority in religious matters.

Saito: I think we should consider the distinction between priesthood and laity, between professional clerics and lay practitioners, not as one of essence but of function; not as one of rank but of roles.

Ikeda: We have no class of professional clerics in the SGI. Our members—all of whom live in the secular world—not only study Buddhist doctrine but are responsible for propagating the Daishonin's teachings and performing various ceremonies and religious services. Ours is a religion in which ordinary people assume full responsibility.

The founder and first president of the Soka Gakkai,

Tsunesaburo Makiguchi, called on us to be active practitioners, not passive believers, and we have rallied to his call.

In traditional religious institutions, a small group of professional clerics monopolizes authority, while the lay believers are called on to follow. That type of organization is definitely no longer appropriate to contemporary society as we approach the twenty-first century.

Endo: Even the Roman Catholic Church, which is governed by its priests, is beginning to grant substantial authority to lay believers, and their voices are having a profound effect on the institution as a whole. Religious bodies are moving irrevocably toward an increased respect for the laity and a broader recognition of its role.

The churches of the Japan Baptist Convention are another example. They have abolished their ministerial policy entirely. Twenty-five years ago, theologian Yoshinobu Kumazawa wrote of this development:

> The minister, ensconced in his role in the clergy, knows the contradictions and changes of society only indirectly, through the believers. He does not confront them directly…. Sermons created by one who has no direct experience of the anxieties and sufferings borne by ordinary people in their daily lives will, naturally, not reach others' hearts. Nor is there any opportunity for believers to challenge such sermons. A faith that changes society will not be stirred in the hearts of followers who only obey the authority of such ministers and remain spiritually dependent on them.[8]

Since that passage was written, the idea of creating a lay Christianity, centered on the laity instead of the ministry, has been proposed by ministers themselves.

Ikeda: Only those out in the world who struggle daily with life's realities understand others who face the same struggles. Inevitably, if religion is to make a serious attempt to open itself to the people, it must move away from an organization centered on a privileged class to one where the people are central.

Suda: "Is a priesthood necessary?" Zao Puchu, president of the Chinese Buddhist Association, has discussed this question. He concludes: "If one observes the causes and conditions of the Buddhist teaching and the causes and conditions of benefiting all living beings, it is not necessary to become a priest."[9] He continues: "Priests cannot assume the role of the individual in praying for blessings and preventing disasters, nor can they assume the role of God in granting blessings and forgiving sins."[10] And he observes: "Historically speaking, Buddhism did not flourish in the periods when there were the greatest number of priests. In fact, when there were too many priests, Buddhism declined."[11]

Ikeda: Dr. Zao has been a friend of mine since my first visit to China in 1974. He is a very well-known calligrapher and the vice chairman of the Chinese People's Political Consultative Conference.

We have discussed the Lotus Sutra together many times and for many hours, in China and in Tokyo. He is a master of each word and phrase of the text. When I say, "At that time the World-Honored One," he replies with what comes next, "calmly arose from his samadhi"[12] (LS2, 23).

Saito: Four years ago, as a member of the First SGI Youth Cultural Exchange Delegation to China, I was fortunate to visit Mount Tiantai (Jpn T'ien-t'ai), where the great Chinese Buddhist teacher T'ien-t'ai lived.

Ikeda: It is the place of which Nichiren Daishonin writes, "On Mount T'ien-t'ai there is a place called the Dragon Gate, which is a waterfall a thousand feet in height" (WND, 1021).

Saito: Yes. It's now called the Stone Bridge Waterfall. Halfway up the waterfall a bridge spans it, and looking up from the bottom of the falls, it really does appear as if a dragon were rising through a stone gate. At a nearby ancient site, a plaque with calligraphy by President Zao reads: "May the Law Prosper Throughout the Ages." The bold strokes of the calligraphy vividly communicate his wish that Buddhism enrich and nourish the people forever.

Ikeda: Time and again, Dr. Zao has said to me: "Buddhism was originally closely connected to the people. That is why it is right for Buddhists to go out among the people." He also told me: "When I visited Japan, I was shown a film of one of your culture festivals. I was deeply impressed by the vibrant energy of the participants, clear proof that the SGI is active among the people." He sees the members of the SGI—a lay Buddhist organization—as manifesting the fundamental spirit of Buddhism to work among the people.

   Religion in the twenty-first century must provide people with the wisdom to be independent, to think and decide wisely for themselves how to live their lives.

Suda: Religion must move beyond its tendency to keep people in a childlike state, without the ability to think for themselves. Dr. Harvey Cox, chairman of the Department of Applied Theology at Harvard University's School of Divinity, emphasized this point in an article he contributed to the *Seikyo Shimbun.*[13]

   In his book *The Seduction of the Spirit,* Dr. Cox writes, "In the final analysis it is always [ordinary people] who are the real bearers of religion."[14]

Ikeda: Dr. Cox went to school with American civil rights leader Dr. Martin Luther King Jr. The two met during the bus boycott that began when Rosa Parks bravely refused to give up her seat to a white passenger in Montgomery, Alabama, in December 1955.

Endo: They belonged to the same Baptist church and remained comrades in the nonviolent struggle for civil rights for more than twelve years, until Dr. King was assassinated. They even spent time in prison together.

Ikeda: I will never forget Dr. Cox's words the first time we spoke at Soka University [on May 2, 1992]. He stated that the ideals for which Dr. King lived and died were at one with the philosophy of Buddhism, on which the SGI is based. He went on to say that his personal goal was to realize that ideal, that system of values, in his own life.

Saito: Dr. Cox studied Christianity. In spite of the differences between the two religions, he felt a great affinity with Buddhism. Whether people have a prejudiced or a correct view of life cannot be measured by their religious denominations or to what doctrines they subscribe.

Ikeda: Nichiren Daishonin writes that some people come to a correct view of life through systems of thought and philosophies other than Buddhism. One who encounters the Lotus Sutra but is prejudiced and does not try to comprehend its true greatness is inferior, he asserts, to the wise men and saints of non-Buddhist teachings. He also writes, "When one knows the Lotus Sutra, one understands the meaning of all worldly affairs" (WND, 76).

The wisdom of the Lotus Sutra is a wisdom that improves society and brings happiness to the people. Unless it accomplishes those things, it is not real Buddhist wisdom. From a broader perspective, I think we can say all wisdom that improves the lot of the people, that contributes to their happiness, is the wisdom of the Lotus Sutra.

The Daishonin wrote of the ancient Chinese statesmen T'ai-kung Wang[15] and Chang Liang,[16] who defeated tyrants and brought relief to the people: "Though these men lived before the introduction of Buddhism, they helped the people as emissaries of Shakyamuni Buddha, the lord of teachings. And though the adherents of the non-Buddhist scriptures were unaware of it, the wisdom of such men contained at heart the wisdom of Buddhism" (WND, 1121–22).

He is saying that even before Buddhism reached China, these individuals were applying Buddhist wisdom to help the people. Being based on the people is the same as being based on humanity. This focus on the welfare of humanity shines with a brilliance that transcends sectarianism and distinctions of priesthood and laity.

"What can I, an ordinary human being, do for others, for society?" That is the spirit of the Lotus Sutra. A religion for the people in the twenty-first century must be an inexhaustible source of such awareness and the energy to carry it out.

The poet of the people, Walt Whitman, writes:

> *Why what have you thought of yourself?*
> *Is it you then that thought yourself less?*
> *Is it you that thought the President greater than you?*
> *Or the rich better off than you? or the educated wiser than you?*[17]

And in another poem:

> *What do you suppose I would intimate to you in a hundred*
>   *ways, but that man or woman is as good as God?*
> *And that there is no God any more divine than Yourself?*[18]

"Yourself" here can also be read as life—this is the realm of Buddhism and the world of the Lotus Sutra. Nothing is greater or worthier of respect than you yourself—this is the message that the Lotus Sutra calls out to every individual.

NOTES

1. Hajime Nakamura, *Niso no Kokuhaku* (Confession of Nuns) (Tokyo: Iwanami Bunko, 1982), p. 120. A Japanese translation of the Pali text Therigatha.

2. *Vinaya-Pitaka*, "Mahavagga."

3. Kumarajiva's Chinese Lotus Sutra translation is the text upon which Nichiren Daishonin based his studies and which is used in the liturgy of gongyo. The English translation by Burton Watson, *The Lotus Sutra*, is also based on this text.

4. The Buddha's thirty-two features and eighty characteristics: Attributes described in the provisional teachings. These unusual qualities awed the people, who then sought the Buddha and aspired to Buddhahood. They signify the Buddha's wisdom, ability, compassion, etc.

5. Magadha: India's most powerful kingdom during the time of Shakyamuni. It was ruled during his lifetime by Bimbisara, followed by his son Ajatashatru. Later, in the third century B.C., King Ashoka ruled this region, which included Rajagriha, Eagle Peak and the Bamboo Grove Monastery.

6. Kyosei Hayashima, *Shoki Bukkyo to Shakai Seikatsu* (Early Buddhism and Social Life), (Tokyo: Iwanami Shoten, 1964), p. 471.

7. *Fuji Nikko Shonin Shoden* (Detailed Biography of Nikko Shonin and the Fuji School), p. 703.

8. Yoshinobu Kumazawa, *Asu no Shingaku to Kyodai* (Future Theology and the Church), (Tokyo: Nihon Kisho Kyodan Shuppankyoku [Publishing Division of the United Church of Christ, Japan], 1974), p. 19.

9. Translated from Chinese: Zao Puchu, *Bukkyo Nymon* (Introduction to Buddhism), trans. Yuan Hui, (Tokyo: Hozokan, 1992), p. 78.

10. Ibid., p. 80.

11. Ibid., p. 84.

12. *Samadhi*: A state of intense concentration of the mind, which produces a sense of inner serenity.

13. In the *Seikyo Shimbun* column "Opinions From Scholars and Social Critics—On Religion in the Twenty-First Century," February 28, 1995.

14. Harvey Cox, *The Seduction of the Spirit: The Use and Misuse of People's Religion*, (New York: Simon and Schuster, 1973), p. 144.

15. T'ai-kung Wang: Teacher and advisor of Hsi Po, the Earl of the West (later known as King Wen of the Chou dynasty). His strategies are said to have enabled Hsi Po's son, King Wu, to overthrow the Yin dynasty and establish the Chou dynasty.

16. Chang Liang (d. 168 B.C.E.): A statesman and strategist who assisted Liu Pang in the overthrow of the Ch'in dynasty and the establishment of the Han dynasty.

17. Walt Whitman, "A Song for Occupations," *Leaves of Grass*, (New York: Dutton, 1968), p. 179.

18. Ibid., "Law for Creations," p. 322.

PART TWO

"Introduction" Chapter

4 *"This Is What I Heard":*
The Pulse of the Oneness
of Mentor and Disciple

Saito: In 1995, the Saint-Petersburg Branch of the Institute of Oriental Studies of the Russian Academy of Sciences presented you, President Ikeda, with a microfilm copy of the Lotus Sutra in the Western Xia (Xi Xia, or Tangut) script. I understand that this is the first time this important manuscript, which many scholars around the world have been waiting to study, has been made public.

Ikeda: I am very honored to receive it. As the founder of the Institute of Oriental Philosophy here in Tokyo, I have high hopes for the development of greater cooperation between the two research institutions.

Western Xia was a kingdom established by the Tangut, a people of Tibetan stock, in what is now northwestern China. Buddhism was the predominant religion. The kingdom flourished from the eleventh through the early thirteenth centuries, and in the short two centuries of its existence, Western Xia developed its own writing system, the Tangut script, and translated numerous Buddhist sutras.

The Tangut-script Lotus Sutra that I received was based on the Chinese translation by the great Kumarajiva with which we are so familiar. The ancient city of Dunhuang, famous as a center of Buddhism and Buddhist art, was also once a part of Western Xia.

Suda: When I think of the people of Western Xia reading the Lotus Sutra, I feel a sense of closeness and affinity with them. Also, I am rather curious about how they understood this scripture and how they studied Buddhism.

Endo: A Western Xia proverb can be translated: "The wise person speaks gently and wins others' allegiance, just as the Yellow River flows serenely and carries all with it."[1]

Saito: "Gently" does not mean a superficial show of courtesy but a genuine sincerity.

Ikeda: Yes, it means an open, considerate attitude; a broadness of heart, a warmth that embraces others. Though the content of one's words may be harsh or strict, when based on such genuine sincerity, they are in fact words of gentleness.

The meaning of this proverb would seem to be this: Wise people speak clearly and reasonably; that is why they can enable people to grasp and accept what they are saying — much like the Yellow River, which flows powerfully while carrying many people gently upon its waters.

The people of Western Xia were undoubtedly intelligent, forthright and proud. We Japanese, who tend to lack conviction and to be taken in easily by devious rhetoric, should look to them as a model.

Now let us proceed on our journey through the Lotus Sutra just like the Yellow River, moving forward with steady momentum. We at last begin our discussion of the first chapter, "Introduction."

Saito: As the name indicates, this is the opening chapter. Its content can be divided into three major parts.

The first part opens with "This is what I heard" (LS1, 3) and then introduces the congregation of myriad sentient beings assembled on Mount Gridhrakuta (Eagle Peak) at Rajagriha.

Suda: "This is what I heard" — or "Thus I heard" as it is also often translated—appears at the beginning of almost every sutra. It's a sort of set phrase, isn't it?

Ikeda: Yes, but in the case of the Lotus Sutra, the act of hearing has deep meaning, and it is emphasized throughout the scripture. Therefore, although "This is what I heard" is a standard in most sutras, it is especially significant in the case of the Lotus Sutra. This is an important point, one profoundly relevant to Nichiren Daishonin's Buddhism.

Saito: The second part of "Introduction" is when Shakyamuni enters "the samadhi of the place of immeasurable meanings" (LS1, 5) and manifests a variety of extraordinary phenomena.

Suda: "The samadhi of the place of immeasurable meanings" refers to a state of meditation in which one concentrates his or her mind on the fundamental Law that is the source of the Buddha's innumerable teachings.

Ikeda: The name of this meditation implies that the Lotus Sutra, which the Buddha is about to expound, is the ultimate teaching that all other teachings are based on or derive from. The Sutra of Immeasurable Meanings, which serves as a prologue to the Lotus Sutra, states, "Immeasurable meanings derive from a single Law." This single, ultimate teaching is revealed in the Lotus Sutra.

Endo: It is not until the "Expedient Means" chapter that Shakyamuni calmly arises from his meditation and actually begins to preach the Lotus Sutra. The first chapter is devoted instead to describing the array of wondrous phenomena Shakyamuni manifests with his transcendental powers while in his state of intense meditation.

Suda: For example, *mandarava* and *manjushaka* flowers rain down from the heavens on the Buddha and the assembly, and the earth shakes and trembles in six ways. As a result, the beings gathered on Eagle Peak are delighted beyond what they have ever experienced; they rejoice and gaze intently at the Buddha. The Buddha then emits a ray of light from the tuft of white hair[2] between his eyebrows, completely illuminating the eighteen thousand lands to the east.

Ikeda: Simply hearing this episode may cause a person to think that the Lotus Sutra is some kind of fairy tale or, in today's terms, a science-fiction story!

Concerning the beings who gathered on Eagle Peak in the "Introduction" chapter, President Toda once wrote:

> There were twelve thousand voice-hearers headed by Shariputra; eighty thousand bodhisattvas; Yashodhara,[3] who was accompanied by six thousand of her followers and retainers; Ajatashatru,[4] along with several thousand of his followers and retainers; and each of the eight kinds of nonhuman beings [heavenly beings, dragons, *yakshas, gandharvas, asuras, garudas, kimnaras, mahoragas*] brought their followers and retainers, numbering in the tens of thousands. The roughest calculation shows that hundreds of thousands must have attended the assembly at Eagle Peak.
>
> There were eighty thousand bodhisattvas and twelve thousand voice-hearers alone! How is it possible that, in an age without microphones, Shakyamuni assembled an audience of such huge proportions and spoke to them all? The Lotus Sutra tells us that indeed they did all gather and hear him preach. An enormous number of listeners —hundreds of thousands—gathered and heard Shakyamuni expound the Law. Is that a lie? No, it is not. Did that many really assemble? How was it possible for the Buddha to lecture to such a vast body of listeners without a microphone, no matter how loudly he spoke?...

> The Lotus Sutra says that the gathering lasted eight years. With that many gathered for eight years, providing food for them all would have been a monumental task. What would they have done about organizing toilets for such a crowd? But does the sutra lie? No, it does not. They assembled, and yet they did not assemble....
>
> Those gathered were the voice-hearers and the bodhisattvas who dwelled within Shakyamuni's own life. Hence, there is nothing to hinder even tens of millions of such voice-hearers and bodhisattvas from assembling.[5]

Mr. Toda didn't want to make the Lotus Sutra seem like some fanciful story divorced from reality or Buddhism, some kind of abstraction. Moreover, he was absolutely convinced that the Lotus Sutra and Buddhism were neither. He knew the Lotus Sutra was in fact the Law of life, the Law existing in the depths of one's own being.

From this perspective, then, we see that the ray of light emanating from the tuft of white hair between the Buddha's eyebrows and illuminating the lands to the east represents the profound truth of life. In the "Record of the Orally Transmitted Teachings," the Daishonin says, "The light from the white tuft of hair is Nam-myoho-renge-kyo" (GZ, 712). Precisely because it is the light of the Mystic Law, it illuminated all worlds, from the hell of incessant suffering (Avichi hell) to the highest heavenly realm (Akanishtha heaven). The Mystic Law has the power to lead even those in the hell of incessant suffering to enlightenment.

Endo: Each of the worlds illuminated by that light is described in vivid detail, as if we were watching an epic film. The Buddhas of various lands are preaching, and those who have embraced the teachings are practicing them in many ways. In some lands, the Buddha has died, and his followers, out of love and respect for him, erect stupas or memorial towers as offerings of faith.

Ikeda: Yes, it is a movie on a truly colossal scale projected on the screen of the whole universe. The entire cosmos is the stage of the Lotus Sutra. All Buddhas have attained their enlightenment based on the Mystic Law, and it is the Lotus Sutra that reveals this one fundamental Law—the Mystic Law. As a prelude to the presentation of this great Law, a variety of startling omens occur. [In reference to this point, the Lotus Sutra reads:]

> At the time Manjushri said…:"I suppose that the Buddha, the World-Honored One, wishes now to expound the great Law, to rain down the rain of the great Law, to blow the conch of the great Law, to beat the drum of the great Law, to elucidate the meaning of the great Law…. He wishes to cause all living beings to hear and understand the Law, which is difficult for all the world to believe. Therefore he has manifested this auspicious portent [of emitting a beam of light from the white tuft of hair between his eyebrows]." (LS1, 13–14)

Saito: The third and final part of "Introduction" is devoted to the description of these auspicious omens. Bodhisattva Maitreya, representing all the assembled listeners, voices surprise and doubts by asking why Shakyamuni has manifested all these astounding phenomena. Bodhisattva Manjushri replies to Maitreya's questions.

In doing so, Manjushri speaks of experiences in previous lives. He describes how in the past a Buddha named Sun Moon Bright manifested the same kind of wondrous phenomena when he preached the Lotus Sutra. On that basis, says Manjushri, Shakyamuni must also be about to preach the Lotus Sutra.

A UNIVERSAL LOTUS SUTRA

Ikeda: Both the ultimate teaching preached by the Buddha Sun Moon Bright and the teaching Shakyamuni was about to preach were the Lotus Sutra. This is an important point.

In the same chapter, Manjushri goes on to say that in addition to the Buddha Sun Moon Bright whom he had encountered in a past lifetime, there were twenty thousand Buddhas named Sun Moon Bright before that, implying that the ultimate great teaching all of those Buddhas taught was the Lotus Sutra. Nor does it not stop there.

In the "Parable of the Phantom City" chapter, the Buddha Great Universal Wisdom Excellence preaches the Lotus Sutra, and in the "The Bodhisattva Never Disparaging" chapter, Buddha Awesome Sound King does so as well.

After the death of the Buddha Sun Moon Bright, his disciple Bodhisattva Wonderfully Bright preaches the Lotus Sutra. After the passing of the Buddha Great Universal Wisdom Excellence, his sixteen bodhisattva disciples preach the Lotus Sutra, too. After the passing of the Buddha Awesome Sound King, Bodhisattva Never Disparaging recites the so-called twenty-four–character Lotus Sutra.[6] The Lotus Sutra is always a teaching for the time after the Buddha's passing.

The sutra also relates that the various Lotus Sutras preached by these Buddhas of the past were of enormous length. The Lotus Sutra of the Buddha Sun Moon Bright was preached over the incredibly long period of sixty small kalpas.[7] The Lotus Sutra of the Buddha Awesome Sound King comprised "twenty thousand, ten thousand, a million verses" (LS20, 267), while the Lotus Sutra of the Buddha Great Universal Wisdom Excellence was preached for more than eight thousand kalpas and contained verses as numerous as the grains of sand of the Ganges River.

What all this means is that the Lotus Sutra is not only Shakyamuni's twenty-eight–chapter Lotus Sutra that we know and read today. Though the forms in which they were preached are different, all of them are the Lotus Sutra.

Saito: That would lead us to conclude that there is a universal Lotus Sutra.

Ikeda: Yes. Mr. Toda, who had grasped its very essence, offers a noteworthy perspective on the Lotus Sutra:

> The same Lotus Sutra is expressed in different ways, depending on the Buddha who preaches it, the time it is preached, and the capacity of the people to understand it. Though the ultimate truth of the Lotus Sutra is identical in all cases, there will be differences in its presentation according to whether the living beings of a particular time have a strong or weak connection to Buddhism.
>
> The average person with a slight knowledge of Buddhism will think that only Shakyamuni has preached the Lotus Sutra. But in fact the Lotus Sutra tells us that Bodhisattva Never Disparaging and the Buddha Great Universal Wisdom Excellence also taught the Lotus Sutra. And the Great Teacher T'ien-t'ai also taught it.[8]

The ultimate truth is one, but it is expressed in many forms, and all of them are the Lotus Sutra. The universal Lotus Sutra is the teaching in which the Buddha reveals and makes accessible to all people the Law he has become enlightened to, the Law for attaining Buddhahood, so that all may achieve true happiness and ease.

Nichiren Daishonin spoke of the Lotus Sutra in terms of its comprehensive, abbreviated and essential forms. The essential form of the Lotus Sutra was his own Nam-myoho-renge-kyo, and the practice most appropriate for today is this essential Lotus Sutra.

The Daishonin doesn't specifically identify the comprehensive and abbreviated forms of the Lotus Sutra, but if we think of the enormous and lengthy versions of the Lotus Sutra preached by the past Buddhas as the comprehensive form, then the twenty-eight–chapter version would be the abbreviated form. Or, if we regard the twenty-eight–chapter version as the comprehensive form, Bodhisattva Never Disparaging's twenty-four–character Lotus Sutra would be the abbreviated form.

Mr. Toda also spoke of three kinds of Lotus Sutras: (1) the twenty-eight chapters of the Lotus Sutra, (2) T'ien-t'ai's treatise *Great Concentration and Insight* and (3) Nichiren Daishonin's Nam-myoho-renge-kyo.

Saito: Though we may be straying a bit from the subject, I think the view of the Lotus Sutra existing in many differing versions sheds light on the question as to whether the twenty-eight–chapter Lotus Sutra actually contains the direct teaching of Shakyamuni himself or is in fact the creation of later editors and compilers. In other words, could we regard the core thought of the Lotus Sutra as Shakyamuni's direct teaching but still say the form in which that thought is presented reflects the conditions of the times in which the sutra was compiled?

Ikeda: I think we can say that Shakyamuni's thought, which forms the sutra's core, assumed a certain shape in response to the conditions of the time and the prevailing state of philosophical thought when the sutra was compiled.

The age sought Shakyamuni's thought, and Shakyamuni's thought appeared in response to that need. What we see at work here is the mutual response, or communion, between the people and the Buddha. This is how a universal philosophy comes into being. We could also describe it as the living dynamism of a true philosophy. Though the philosophy may appear in a new form, it does so because that form articulates the truth of the philosophy better in that particular circumstance of time. In that sense, I believe we can answer the question you posed earlier, about whether the Lotus Sutra is the direct teaching of Shakyamuni or a creation of its compilers, by saying it is the direct teaching of the Buddha.

Of course, the form in which the teaching finds expression reflects the historical circumstances of the period in which it was compiled, and historical research into that period can reveal much about the sutra. We should welcome the results of sound academic research. I am also convinced such research can do nothing to undermine the philosophical value of the Lotus Sutra, and that in fact any fresh revelations will only make it shine all the more brilliantly.

Suda: Many scholars today support the theory that the Lotus Sutra was compiled around the first century CE, several hundred years after Shakyamuni's death.

At that time, the different schools of Theravada Buddhism had come to think of themselves as the orthodox lineage of Buddhism and had become closed, authoritarian and divorced from the people. Against that background, a movement to express faith in the Buddha by worshiping or erecting stupas dedicated to him arose among the laity. Their faith led them to try to establish direct communication with the Buddha rather than accepting the authoritarian monks as intermediaries. This became the Mahayana Buddhist movement, and scriptures such as the Wisdom sutras, the Flower Garland Sutra and the Lotus Sutra were compiled at this time.

The Theravada schools criticized the new Mahayana movement, saying that the Mahayana scriptures were arbitrary creations and not the teaching of the Buddha. The criticism that Mahayana is not the Buddha's teaching existed from the Mahayana movement's very inception.

Endo: The new Mahayana movement must have seemed like a sham, a fraudulent new religion to the Theravada traditionalists.

Even though centuries had passed since Shakyamuni's death, however, it does not follow that the new Mahayana scriptures were arbitrary fictions with no link to him. They may have been recorded many years later, but it is quite possible they were the Buddha's teachings handed down as part of the oral transmission. This is true not only of the Lotus Sutra but of the other Mahayana sutras set down in writing at about this time.

Even the Theravada scriptures were recorded by Shakyamuni's disciples only after his death.

Ikeda: In ancient India, it seems to have been customary not to write down important teachings but to memorize and transmit them orally. The great Buddhist scholar Nagarjuna[9] writes in his *Treatise on the Great Perfection of Wisdom:* "The Buddha's disciples recited the Buddha's teachings and recorded them as scriptures." These "scriptures" are the Mahayana sutras.

Be that as it may, we can only praise the genius of the Lotus Sutra's compilers, for they could extract the essence of Shakyamuni's thought from the teachings handed down both orally and in writing and magnificently restore that essence to life. I can't help thinking that among the compilers, some brilliant individual pursued and grasped Shakyamuni's enlightenment and demonstrated superlative leadership in setting down the sutra in writing.

Suda: As research on Buddhist texts proceeds, scholars have discovered the seedlings of later Mahayana teachings in the earliest Theravada texts and have come to emphasize that indeed the Mahayana resulted from developing the Buddha's ideas in a correct and orthodox fashion. Clearly, then, the assertion that only the Theravada scriptures are the Buddha's teachings and the Mahayana scriptures are not is no longer tenable. Both Theravada and Mahayana scriptures derive from a single source: Shakyamuni.

Saito: Of all the Mahayana scriptures, the Lotus Sutra is unparalleled in its faith and wisdom to seek Shakyamuni. In some respects, it might even be called a first-century treatise on Shakyamuni.

THE SIGNIFICANCE OF "THIS IS WHAT I HEARD"

Saito: I think we can also interpret the significance of "This is what I heard," the opening of the "Introduction" chapter, from the standpoint of the universal Lotus Sutra. The issue is what "this" refers to, in other words, the actual content of "what I heard." On the surface, of course, it is the twenty-eight chapters of the Lotus Sutra, but it goes much further than that.

Endo: The Great Teacher Miao-lo interprets what was heard, or "the substance of a doctrine heard from the Buddha," in a conventional way as the entire twenty-eight chapters. But Nichiren Daishonin went further, declaring that "the substance of a doctrine" refers to "the heart of all phenomena" (GZ, 709), in other words, to Myoho-renge-kyo.

Explaining this in the "Record of the Orally Transmitted Teachings," the Daishonin cites the following statement by T'ien-t'ai in his *Words and Phrases of the Lotus Sutra*: "'This' [of 'This is what I heard'] indicates 'the substance of a doctrine heard from the Buddha,' while 'what I heard' indicates 'a person who can uphold that doctrine'" (GZ, 709).

Ikeda: In this case, the Daishonin applies the principle of 'text, meaning and intent' to reading the sutra. "Text" refers to the sutra's literal content. "Meaning" indicates the doctrine or principle to which the text refers. When we restrict ourselves to examining only the literal text of the scripture, we can only get as far as its meaning.

But no amount of discussion of the text and meaning of the Lotus Sutra will be truly valuable unless we get to its heart, or true intent. The Daishonin concludes that "'the substance of a doctrine' indicates Nam-myoho-renge-kyo" (GZ, 709).

"The substance of a doctrine," "the heart of all phenomena," is the Buddha's wisdom itself, which pulsates through all twenty-eight chapters of the sutra. That wisdom is Nam-myoho-renge-kyo. "This is what I heard"—in other words, having heard that wisdom just as it is—refers to faith and the way of mentor and disciple. Only through the disciples' faith in the mentor can they enter the world of the Buddha's wisdom. As T'ien-t'ai stated in his *Great Concentration and Insight*, and Nagarjuna in his *Treatise on the Great Perfection of Wisdom*, "Buddhism is like an ocean that one can only enter with faith" (WND, 832).

From this perspective, "This is what I heard," in terms of the Lotus Sutra, means to concentrate one's entire being on apprehending and connecting with the vibration of the Buddha's life. "This" refers to the faith and understanding that enable those who hear the teachings to "hear them exactly as they are preached" and engrave them in their lives. Since this activity involves one's entire being, the expression "I heard" is used. "I," the entire being, "hear," not just the ears.

The "I" in this phrase is usually taken to mean Ananda,[10] the disciple of Shakyamuni said to have been central in compiling the scriptures. Today, in the Latter Day of the Law, however, "I" signifies each of us. We each listen to the Daishonin's teaching of Nam-myoho-renge-kyo with our whole being and embrace faith in it. This is the true meaning of "This is what I heard."

As Nichiren Daishonin says: "The meaning behind every word and phrase of the twenty-eight chapters of the sutra refers to the hearing of this doctrine as it applies to oneself, and this is summed up in the expression 'This is what I heard.' What is heard is Nam-myoho-renge-kyo. Therefore, the sutra says 'all attain the Buddha way'" (GZ, 794).

We are not to read the sutra as something separate from ourselves. Instead, we should "hear" it as it applies to oneself and as the Law of our own lives.

Endo: That is a very clear explanation.

In his *Treatise on the Great Perfection of Wisdom*, Nagarjuna writes, "The meaning of 'this' [of 'This is what I heard'] is faith." And T'ien-t'ai writes in his *Words and Phrases of the Lotus Sutra*, "'This' indicates to have faith in and follow [the teachings of the sutra just as they are]."

Nagarjuna uses an interesting allegory to describe faith. Faith, he says, is like soft leather, while lack of faith is like stiff leather. Soft leather can be put to many uses, but stiff leather cannot. In other words, those with faith follow the Buddha's teachings and hear them just as they are, while those without faith cannot.

T'ien-t'ai's "to have faith in and follow" is very significant, I think. He further states that "follow" here means that "one proceeds to follow the Buddha's teaching as a student follows the instructions of his teacher." When one follows in this way, the path of mentor and disciple is established.

Ikeda: The essence of "This is what I heard" is the oneness of mentor and disciple, and that is the quintessence of the transmission of Buddhism.

The drama of the oneness of mentor and disciple, in which there is a mutual resonance and response between the Buddha's resolve to save all living things and the resolve of the disciple who seeks to embody and propagate the Buddha's teaching, is epitomized in this expression, "This is what I heard."

Further, the Lotus Sutra is a scripture for the time after the Buddha's death. How are sentient beings to be saved after the Buddha dies? Who at that time will uphold and propagate the sutra? These basic themes already begin to be played out in "Introduction." One example is the account of how Bodhisattva Wonderfully Bright, the disciple of the Buddha Sun Moon Bright, preached the Lotus Sutra after his mentor's passing and brought others to enlightenment, starting with Sun Moon Bright's eight princely sons.

Saito: Buddhas wish to help all beings throughout eternity attain enlightenment, and that is the very purpose for their appearance in the world.

Ikeda: Yes. The Daishonin writes, "If Nichiren's compassion is truly great and encompassing, Nam-myoho-renge-kyo will spread for ten thousand years and more, for all eternity..." (WND, 736).

It is also true in general that those who really care for the people retain the power to move people even after their death. Mahatma Gandhi, for instance, once declared that if his soul could serve as a light for humanity, then he would continue speaking even from the grave.

The struggle of disciples who share their mentor's passionate determination to save others far into the future does indeed contribute to doing just that. The Law truly does give rise to compassionate action. Things may be all right while one's mentor is still present. But it is when the mentor has gone that the bond between mentor and disciple is truly tested. Buddhism is that strict.

When all were mourning after Shakyamuni died, one old monk said: "Stop, my friends. Do not be sad. Do not lament. We have been well freed from that great practitioner. He was always pestering us, telling us it is good to do this, it is wrong to do that. From now on, let us do as we please. And let us not do what we do not wish to do."[11]

I am sure you are appalled by the sentiments of this old monk. But in fact, that is how people's minds work. Therefore, your mission as leaders of the twenty-first century is extremely important.

Saito: Yes, we really need to remember this.

Returning to "Introduction," after the death of Buddha Sun Moon Bright, his disciple Bodhisattva Wonderfully Bright preached the Lotus Sutra in the same way Sun Moon Bright had done. Should we regard this as the practice of "This is what I heard"?

Ikeda: Yes, I believe so. The Buddha's passing was a turning point at which Bodhisattva Wonderfully Bright was transformed from a disciple who sought to be led to enlightenment into a disciple who led others to enlightenment. This is the spirit of the Lotus Sutra.

The heart of "This is what I heard" exists in the disciples rising up with the determination to lead others to happiness just as their mentor did. It is a declaration of a momentous struggle, of readily taking on all hardships in the cause of guiding others toward enlightenment.

The compilation of the twenty-eight–chapter Lotus Sutra after Shakyamuni's death was made possible by his disciples who shared with one another "This is what I heard," out of their wish, based on the same state of life as the Buddha, to save all people. In this sense, the Lotus Sutra is an embodiment of the spirit of the oneness of mentor and disciple.

Perhaps from one perspective, Mr. Toda's enlightenment in prison, too, can be described as his personal experience of "This is what I heard" while undergoing persecution for the sake the Law. There, he "heard" the sutra's words "I am always here, preaching the Law" (LS16, 229) as expounded by the original Buddha, Nichiren Daishonin.

Suda: Speaking of disciples rising up to carry on their mentor's mission, I recently reread some passages from your *A Youthful Diary*, dated after Mr. Toda's death [on April 2, 1958], and I was moved once again by their message. Your journal entries depict how, making your mentor's spirit your own, you struggled and racked your brains day after day to find the best way to protect and develop the Soka Gakkai. Please allow me to quote a few excerpts:

> April 8, 1958: Approximately 120,000 people came to offer incense today [in memory of Mr. Toda]. Sincere people who heartily respect Sensei. Determined that I must guide them further from here on, limitlessly, toward happiness. On behalf of my "father."...
>
> May 25, 1958: Sometimes feel indignant at many of the leaders. Have they forgotten Sensei's death? Regrettable....
>
> November 10, 1958: Every day, I feel my late mentor's compassion flowing and pulsating within my being....
>
> December 12, 1958: The youth are moving ahead dynamically. Will fight for them, throughout my life, sacrificing myself if need be. This is precisely what my mentor did....
>
> February 20, 1959: The cry that issued from the life of my mentor must not be allowed to fade as the days pass. It must never die out. We have the organization, doctrinal study, social standing...but what's important

is compassion—people of compassion; unflagging seeking spirit, individuals whose resolve to seek the Law knows no bounds....

July 23, 1959: The top leaders should think more seriously about our members. They should abandon their own interests in order to serve the members. Only then will others follow them gladly. Our leaders mustn't become sly or calculating. It would be unfortunate for the members.

Ikeda: I feel exactly the same way today. The spirit of the Lotus Sutra, from start to finish, is that of the oneness of mentor and disciple.

THE SIGNIFICANCE OF HEARING THE LAW: THE VOICE DOES THE BUDDHA'S WORK

Suda: I think hearing has an especially deep significance for human life. We experience sound before we see or smell.

Endo: David Burrows, a New York University music teacher, has some interesting information regarding this. "The unborn child," he says, "may startle in the womb at the sound of a door slamming shut. The rich warm cacophony of the womb has been recorded: the mother's heartbeat and breathing are among the earliest indications babies have of the existence of a world beyond their own skin."[12]

Suda: Hearing seems to be the first of the five senses to develop. In the broadest terms, though, hearing is not simply auditory but also the power of life itself to perceive the mysterious rhythm pulsing throughout the universe.

The Daishonin writes, "This strife-ridden *saha* world is a realm in which enlightenment is achieved through the sense of hearing" (GZ, 415). From my own experience, I can say that I quickly forget what I read in a book, but when I listen carefully to a lecture, the impression it makes on me is many times stronger than reading, and it sticks in my memory.

Endo: The twenty-sixth high priest, Nichikan, said we should continue to chant daimoku for some time after a person has died, so that the departed might hear it.[13]

Saito: In the Lotus Sutra, great importance is placed on hearing the Law. Each time Shakyamuni makes a significant statement on the Law, such as in the "Expedient Means" and "Life Span" chapters, the virtues of hearing the Lotus Sutra are always enumerated immediately afterwards.

Ikeda: Nichiren Daishonin also says, "Hearing is the most important way of comprehending this sutra" (GZ, 416). That is why the voice of the Buddha is so important. With regard to the character *kyo* (sutra) of Myoho-renge-kyo, he says: "The voice does the Buddha's work. This is the meaning of *kyo*" (GZ, 708).

Endo: The Daishonin also says that a "pure and far-reaching voice," a voice that can reach the Brahma heaven, is the foremost among the Buddha's thirty-two remarkable features (WND, 332). The "pure and far-reaching voice" is one that carries far, is clear and pure in tone and is delightful to hear. Shakyamuni's voice must have been such a voice.

Ikeda: I am sure it was because of this marvelous voice that Shakyamuni could inspire people profoundly and revive their spirits. It was a voice of truth embodying the Law for becoming a Buddha that he had become awakened to in the depths of his own being.

The voice is the vibration of the living whole. A person's being and character are revealed by the voice. A French writer once said the voice is our second face. Though we may hide our true appearance, we cannot hide the voice.

Suda: A very interesting article appeared in the British science magazine *Nature* on an experiment about the credibility of various media.[14] Two interviews, one true and one containing falsehoods, were conducted by the same person in three media—print, radio and television. Both interviews were presented in each of these media, and the respective audiences of readers, listeners and viewers were asked to decide which of the two in each medium was false.

Television fooled the most people. But three-fourths of the radio listeners recognized the false story. Newspaper readers fell somewhere in between. I think we can interpret this to mean that though we may be easily fooled by visual images, we are not easily deceived by the voice.

Saito: I sense a marvelous rhythm in the chanting of Nam-myoho-renge-kyo. It is a strong sound that gives people courage and energy.

Suda: The world-renowned violinist Yehudi Menuhin commented on the sound of daimoku in a dialogue with President Ikeda. The *nam* of Nam-myoho-renge-kyo, he said, is a strong sound. The sound *m* is the source of life, the sound that begins the word *mother* and, as the syllable *ma*, the first sound a child learns. This *m* sound is very important, he declared. He added that the significant sound *r* also comes in a crucial, central position in the daimoku (in *renge*).

Ikeda: Daimoku is the fundamental rhythm of the universe, the most revered of all voices. Nichiren Daishonin writes: "[W]hen once we chant Myoho-renge-kyo, with just that single sound we summon forth and manifest the Buddha nature of all Buddhas... and all other living beings. This blessing is immeasurable and boundless" (WND, 887).

He also writes: "We, too, are the eggs of ignorance, which are pitiful things, but when nurtured by the chanting of Nam-myoho-renge-kyo, [we] are free to soar into the sky of the true aspect of all phenomena and the reality of all things" (WND, 1030), and, "Nichiren alone, without sparing his voice, now chants Nam-myoho-renge-kyo, Nam-myoho-renge-kyo" (WND, 736). Not sparing one's voice doesn't refer to loudness or volume. It means the great voice of compassion that seeks to bring all beings to enlightenment.

Without sparing our voices, and with our hearts as one with Nichiren Daishonin, we of the SGI are engaging in activities to propagate the Buddhist teachings.

The SGI resounds with many voices. The most basic voice is our earnest chanting of daimoku. But we also hear the warm voice of encouragement, the vibrant voice of courage, the heartfelt voice of joy, the earnest voice of pledge and commitment, and the clear voice of wisdom. They are the source of an infinite wellspring of benefit.

With all of these unsparing voices, the SGI is performing the glorious work of the Buddha, which is to propagate widely the Mystic Law.

Notes

1. Tatsuo Nishida, *Saika Moji no Hanashi* (A Look at the Tangut Script), (Tokyo: Taishukan Shoten, 1989), p. 167.

2. The tuft of white hair: One of the thirty-two features of a Buddha. A pure, soft tuft of hair curling to the right was said to grow between his eyebrows and constantly emit light.

3. Yashodhara: The wife of Shakyamuni. She was later converted to Buddhism by Shakyamuni and became a nun in the Buddhist Order.

4. Ajatashatru: King of Magadha in Shakyamuni's time. Under his reign, Magadha became the most powerful kingdom in India at that time. Later in life, he converted to Buddhism.

5. Translated from Japanese: *Toda Josei Zenshu,* (Tokyo: Seikyo Shimbunsha, 1986), vol. 6, pp. 591–92.

6. Twenty-four–character Lotus Sutra: "I have profound reverence for you, I would never dare treat you with disparagement or arrogance. Why? Because you are all practicing the bodhisattva way and are sure to attain Buddhahood" (LS20, 266-67). Words that Bodhisattva Never Disparaging spoke to all people; in Chinese, they comprise twenty-four characters, hence the name.

7. Kalpa: (Skt) An extremely long period of time. Sources differ somewhat in their definitions. According to one explanation, the length of a small kalpa is approximately sixteen million years.

8. Translated from Japanese: *Toda Josei Zenshu,* (Tokyo: Seikyo Shimbunsha, 1983), vol. 3, p. 54.

9. Nagarjuna (dates of birth and death unknown): A leading philosopher of the Mahayana movement, active in India from about 150 to 250 A.D. Wrote *Treatise on the Great Perfection of Wisdom.*

10. Ananda: One of Shakyamuni's ten major disciples. He was known as superior in hearing the teachings, and he played a central role in compiling the teachings after the Buddha's passing.

11. *Genshi Bukkyo no Seiritsu* (The Establishment of Early Buddhism), ed. Hajime Nakamura (Tokyo: Shinjusha, 1992), p. 307.

12. David Burrows, *Sound, Speech and Music* (Amherst: University of Massachusetts Press, 1990), p. 17.

13. *Fuji Shugaku Yoshu* (The Selected Works of the Fuji School), (Tokyo: Seikyo Shimbunsha, 1977), vol. 3, p. 264.

14. Richard Wiseman, "The megalab truth test," *Nature*, vol. 373, February 2, 1995, p. 391.

5 "Three Meetings in Two Places": Exchange Between Eternity and the Present Moment

THE GREAT ASSEMBLY: THE CAST OF CHARACTERS

Saito: After the opening "This is what I heard," the "Introduction" chapter continues: "At one time the Buddha was in Rajagriha, staying on Mount Gridhrakuta" (LS1, 3). This tells us where the sutra is being preached—Mount Gridhrakuta, or Eagle Peak, outside the city of Rajagriha,[1] the capital of the ancient kingdom of Magadha. Next, it describes the kinds of beings gathered to hear the Buddha's preaching.

"Introduction" reads:

> At one time the Buddha was in Rajagriha, staying on Mount Gridhrakuta. Accompanying him were a multitude of leading monks numbering twelve thousand persons....
>
> Their names were Ajnata Kaundinya, Mahakashyapa, ...Ananda, and Rahula. All were like these, great arhats who were well known to others.
>
> There were also two thousand persons, some of whom were still learning and some who had completed their learning.
>
> There was the nun Mahaprajapati with her six thousand followers. And there was Rahula's mother, the nun Yashodhara, with her followers.

There were bodhisattvas and mahasattvas, eighty thousand of them....

And there was King Ajatashatru, the son of Vaidehi, with several hundreds of thousands of followers....

Each of these, after bowing in obeisance before the Buddha's feet, withdrew and took a seat to one side. (LS1, 3–5)

Ikeda: As the drama of the Lotus Sutra commences, the setting and characters are introduced.

Suda: I visited Eagle Peak in 1990 as a member of the first SGI Youth Cultural Delegation to India. I expected it to be a solemn, profoundly mystic and sacred site, but it turned out to be a remarkably ordinary rocky peak!

Ikeda: It's not very high, either. According to one source, it was named Eagle Peak because it resembles an eagle's head in shape. Shakyamuni is often said to have preached the Law on its summit.

Endo: The sutra then proceeds to introduce the cast of the assembly in the following order:

(1) Twelve thousand monks who had attained the state of arhat, the highest stage of the voice-hearers. The names of twenty-one arhats are given as representatives of this group, including such well-known disciples of Shakyamuni as Ajnata Kaundinya, Mahakashyapa and Shariputra.

In addition, another two thousand voice-hearers—who either "were still learning" or "had completed their learning"—were also present. Those who "were still learning" were disciples still practicing the three types of learning necessary to attain the state of arhat, namely, the precepts, meditation and wisdom. Those who "had completed their learning" were disciples who had already attained the state of arhat and had nothing more to learn.

(2) The nun Mahaprajapati, Shakyamuni's aunt and stepmother; the nun Yashodhara, Shakyamuni's wife before his renunciation of secular life; and several thousands of their respective followers.

(3) Eighty thousand bodhisattvas. The names of eighteen, including Bodhisattva Manjushri and Bodhisattva Perceiver of the World's Sounds, are listed as representatives of this group.

After our introduction to these voice-hearers and bodhisattvas, we are acquainted with a variety of other sentient beings from the *saha* world who have come to participate in the assembly:

(4) The kings and sons of gods of various heavenly realms, such as Shakra Devanam Indra, the Four Great Heavenly Kings and King Brahma. Their followers totaled anywhere from seventy thousand to eighty thousand, up to well over 100,000, depending on how one calculates.

(5) Eight dragon kings and their followers.

(6) Four *kimnara* kings and their followers.

(7) Four *gandharva* kings and their followers.

(8) Four *asura* kings and their followers.

(9) Four *garuda* kings and their followers.

(10) King Ajatashatru and his followers.

This vast number of beings, which when totaled comes to at least several hundreds of thousands or perhaps even several million, gathered to hear the preaching of the Lotus Sutra.

Ikeda: Yes, it was a huge and extraordinarily diverse gathering. Yet we know that such an enormous number of beings could not possibly have assembled at Eagle Peak all at once.

Suda: My own impression after visiting Eagle Peak is that a hundred people at the most could have sat and listened to Shakyamuni preach at any one time. Being an extremely rocky peak, there is no shade. So remaining there for any length of time during the summer would have been out of the question. When we visited it, one of our Indian guides actually collapsed from the heat.

Ikeda: To reiterate President Toda's observation, which I mentioned in the previous chapter: "Those who gathered [at Eagle Peak for the ceremony of the Lotus Sutra] were the voice-hearers and the bodhisattvas who dwelled within Shakyamuni's own life. Hence, there is nothing to hinder even tens of millions of such voice-hearers and bodhisattvas from assembling."[2]

As he indicates, the Lotus Sutra is an expression of the realm of the Buddha's own life, the world of enlightenment.

Saito: In that sense, we can interpret all the different beings gathered to hear the sutra as symbolizing the different functions and workings inherent in life itself. In terms of the Ten Worlds, the assembly on Eagle Peak comprises beings from the worlds of Bodhisattva, Learning, Heaven, Humanity, Anger, Animality—these six, we can assume, are meant to represent all nine worlds from Hell to Bodhisattva. In other words, the great assembly of the "Introduction" chapter is a manifestation of all beings of the nine worlds enfolded within the Buddha's own life.

Endo: If we interpret it in this fashion, then each member of the great assembly identified in the sutra should have a particular significance. Let's consider a few of the more well-known figures.

Suda: Well, the first name to be mentioned is Ajnata Kaundinya, one of the five ascetics converted by Shakyamuni immediately after the latter attained enlightenment.

Ikeda: Yes, he was Shakyamuni's first disciple. King Ajatashatru, meanwhile, is mentioned last. Guilty of plotting with Devadatta against Shakyamuni, King Ajatashatru came to deeply regret his actions, and toward the end of the Buddha's life he converted to the Buddha's teachings. Perhaps we can regard this listing of Shakyamuni's first and last disciples as a symbolic reference meant to include all the Buddha's disciples during his lifetime.

Saito: When the Daishonin discusses the great assembly in the "Record of the Orally Transmitted Teachings," he, too, talks about Shakyamuni's first and last disciples.

Ikeda: In the "Orally Transmitted Teachings," the Daishonin elucidates the significance of the great assembly in terms of explaining life itself.

The presence of Ajnata Kaundinya, he says, "indicates the principles that 'earthly desires are enlightenment' and 'life and death are nirvana' at work in the lives of us votaries of the Lotus Sutra" (GZ, 710).

Ajatashatru, we may recall, murdered his father, King Bimbisara, attempted to kill his mother, Queen Vaidehi, and plotted against Shakyamuni. The Daishonin describes Ajatashatru's betrayal as an example of the principle that 'the reverse relationship and the positive relationship are ultimately one.' This principle explains that both those who oppose and those who follow the Lotus Sutra can ultimately attain enlightenment. Therefore, even those who commit evil can attain Buddhahood through their reverse relationship formed by slandering the Law when they finally overcome their disbelief in the Lotus Sutra as well as the poisons of greed and ignorance in their lives.

Endo: The other members of the great assembly can also be viewed from a similar perspective.

Suda: We might expect that voice-hearers such as Mahakashyapa and Shariputra would be mentioned at the beginning of the great assembly participants list, since they were leading disciples who historically played a major role in sustaining Shakyamuni's organization. However, right after them, women followers—the nuns Mahaprajapati and Yashodhara—are mentioned. And when King Ajatashatru is mentioned, there is also a reference to his mother, Vaidehi.

Ikeda: The dragon king's daughter's enlightenment in the "Deva-datta" chapter is a well-known example of the Lotus Sutra's teaching that women share the same potential for Buddhahood as men. But that is not the only place in the sutra that this truth is propounded.

In the "Encouraging Devotion" chapter, Shakyamuni prophesies enlightenment for a large number of nuns—of whom Mahaprajapati and Yashodhara are representatives—in a manner confirming what is certain to happen. Both Mahaprajapati and Yashodhara were introduced on an equal footing with male members of the assembly in "Introduction." The enlightenment of women—a distinctive feature of the Lotus Sutra marking a sharp departure from the provisional teachings, which deny this potential—is anticipated from the very first chapter.

Bodhisattva Never Disparaging addresses everyone he encounters, men and women alike, with the promise: "You are all practicing the bodhisattva way and are certain to attain Buddhahood" (LS20, 267). Viewed in its entirety, the Lotus Sutra takes it for granted that there is no distinction between men and women in attaining Buddhahood.

Saito: That is a very important point. Next mentioned are the eighty thousand bodhisattvas, who are praised for their compassionate activities to save others.

Ikeda: First the voice-hearers are mentioned and then the bodhisattvas. Also, when we look at the Lotus Sutra as a whole, in the first nine chapters the assembly representatives to whom Shakyamuni speaks are voice-hearers like Shariputra, but from "Teacher of the Law," the tenth chapter, onward this changes to Bodhisattva Medicine King and other bodhisattvas. Let's discuss this in greater detail later, but suffice it to say for now that this switch from the voice-hearers to the bodhisattvas is an important key to understanding the sutra's message.

Endo: The names of the bodhisattvas in "Introduction" are also quite interesting. While figures such as Bodhisattva Manjushri, Bodhisattva Perceiver of the World's Sounds, Bodhisattva Maitreya and Bodhisattva Medicine King are very well known, mentioned also are the names of relatively unknown bodhisattvas, such as Bodhisattva Constant Exertion, Bodhisattva Never Resting, Bodhisattva Jeweled Palm, Bodhisattva Great Strength and Bodhisattva Jeweled Moon.

Ikeda: We can interpret these bodhisattvas as representing various aspects of the Bodhisattva state. For example, just as their names indicate, Bodhisattva Constant Exertion and Bodhisattva Never Resting are symbolic of an unending struggle for the sake of the Buddhist Law. The name "Never Resting" comes from the Sanskrit *anikshiptadhura,* meaning "one who does not put down a heavy burden."

Suda: The name of Bodhisattva Jeweled Palm means "to hold a treasure," while that of Bodhisattva Brave Donor means "a champion of charity." Bodhisattva Jeweled Moon, Bodhisattva Moonlight and Bodhisattva Full Moon are thought to symbolize the workings of the bodhisattva in illuminating people's lives with the light of diverse wisdom.

Endo: The name of Bodhisattva Maitreya means "compassionate teacher," and that of Bodhisattva Jeweled Accumulation indicates the source of treasures. The name of the last of the bodhisattvas mentioned in "Introduction," Bodhisattva Guiding Leader, indicates a leader of a caravan, representing the leader's function to guide many to enlightenment.

Suda: After the bodhisattvas, various heavenly beings are introduced. The very first is Shakra Devanam Indra, the ruler of the heavens. Indra, originally the Indian god of thunder, was a central deity in ancient Indian mythology.

Endo: The sons of the gods Freedom and Great Freedom trace their origin to Shiva, the ancient Indian god of destruction and a leading deity of Brahmanism. Freedom and Great Freedom seem to have been variant names for this deity.

Even Heavenly King Brahma, the world-creator and supreme deity of Brahmanism, is in attendance with his followers.

Ikeda: The attendance of all of these deities at the preaching of the Lotus Sutra is meant to show that the Buddha is superior to these deities and that he is their teacher and their guide. One title of the Buddha is "Teacher of Gods and Humans," affirming his role as a teacher who can guide heavenly as well as human beings.

It is said that after Shakyamuni attained enlightenment, Brahma asked him to preach the Law. One basic tenet of Buddhism is that the Buddha occupies an infinitely higher place than the various deities of ancient myth and tradition.

Saito: Next, the eight dragon kings are introduced. The dragon kings Nanda, Upananda, Sagara, Vasuki, Takshaka, Anavatapta, Manasvin and Utpalaka are in the assembly, each accompanied by a vast number of followers. It is the daughter of dragon king Sagara who later demonstrates that women, too, can attain enlightenment.

Endo: In addition, various mythical creatures, known as the eight kinds of nonhuman beings, are introduced. The heavenly beings and dragon kings, which we just mentioned, are included in the eight kinds of nonhuman beings, but they are generally treated as a separate category in Buddhist teachings. We can assume this is because, prior to Buddhism, heavenly beings or dragons were the main deities worshiped in ancient India.

Suda: The eight kinds of nonhuman beings are: (1) heavenly beings, beings who inhabit the heavenly realms; (2) dragons, beasts that live in seas and lakes; (3) *yakshas,* a kind of forest-dwelling demon;

(4) *gandharvas*, gods of music that serve King Brahma; (5) *asuras*, a kind of demon that dwells in the sea beneath Mount Sumeru and bears hostility toward heavenly beings; (6) *garudas*, a type of golden bird that preys on dragons; (7) *kimnaras*, gods of music who play musical instruments and whose form is half-human, half-animal; and (8) *mahoragas*, gods with human bodies and the heads of serpents.

Ikeda: The Lotus Sutra is not for human beings alone. It exists to save all living creatures. Interestingly, gods that were worshiped in different localities of ancient India before the birth of Buddhism are described as assembling on Eagle Peak to hear the Lotus Sutra being preached. This is because the new teaching of Buddhism viewed such gods not as external existences governing human lives, as the non–Buddhist teachings had regarded them, but as functions inherent in human life and the life of the universe.

The enlightenment of the Buddha penetrates deeply into the very essence of life, and the Lotus Sutra illuminates the one fundamental Law permeating that essence. That is why the practitioner of the Lotus Sutra is a champion of life who can influence even the heavenly deities. Nichiren Daishonin writes, "Since my heart believes in the Lotus Sutra, I do not fear even Brahma or Shakra..." (WND, 303).

It is also interesting to note that inveterate enemies such as the heavenly beings and *asuras* and the dragons and *garudas* have gathered to hear the sutra. The message here would seem to be: Religions that fan the flames of ethnic hatred are inferior religions. The Lotus Sutra is a teaching of peace and equality.

FROM EAGLE PEAK TO THE CEREMONY IN THE AIR, AND BACK TO EAGLE PEAK

Endo: Now that all of the characters have been introduced, we can discuss the stage upon which they will appear.

Ikeda: Yes. In addition to Eagle Peak, let's also talk about the 'three assemblies in two places.'

Endo: All right. If we look at the overall flow of the Lotus Sutra, the portion beginning with "Introduction" and ending with "The Teacher of the Law," the tenth chapter, is set on Eagle Peak. At the very beginning of "The Emergence of the Treasure Tower," the eleventh chapter, an enormous treasure tower suddenly erupts from the earth and rises to float in the air. Shakyamuni Buddha and Many Treasures Buddha are seated together within the tower, and the assembly is also lifted into the air as the preaching resumes. This Ceremony in the Air continues until "Entrustment," the twenty-second chapter.

In the twenty-third chapter, "Former Affairs of the Bodhisattva Medicine King," the scene returns to Eagle Peak and remains there through the last chapter, "Encouragements of the Bodhisattva Universal Worthy."

Suda: The Lotus Sutra opens and closes on the stage of Eagle Peak, but in the middle, the stage moves into the air. There are thus three assemblies: the first assembly on Eagle Peak, the Ceremony in the Air and the second assembly on Eagle Peak. Hence the designation, the 'three assemblies in two places.'

Saito: While Eagle Peak is a real place where Shakyamuni preached his teachings, the Ceremony in the Air might be described as surreal. The treasure tower described in the Lotus Sutra, for example, is enormous. According to one calculation, it is anywhere from one-third to one-half the size of Earth. Why was it necessary to set this scene so far removed from everyday reality, and why does a treasure tower almost beyond imagination appear? This is a very important point, I think.

Ikeda: Yes, let's explore this in greater detail at another opportunity. Allow me to mention, however, that many Buddhist scholars with whom I have held discussions have shown great interest in the significance of the treasure tower and the Ceremony in the Air.

Endo: Professor Soorya B. Shakya of Nepal has said:

> The Ceremony in the Air is a symbol of the Buddha's immense state of being. All the worlds of the ten directions of the past, as well as all the worlds of the ten directions of the future, are encompassed in that present actuality. The state of Buddhahood transcends time and space. When we awaken to the realm expounded in the Ceremony in the Air, we attain the power to accomplish anything.

Suda: President Toda said the following about the Ceremony in the Air:

> The supremely wondrous state of Buddhahood is latent within each of our lives. The power and nature of this state of life are beyond our imagination and our ability to describe in words. Yet we can manifest this state in our own lives. The ceremony that takes place in "The Emergence of the Treasure Tower" chapter reveals that we, too, can indeed manifest the state of Buddhahood dormant within us.

Ikeda: Mr. Toda taught us clearly what the treasure tower is and the significance of its emergence. That colossal treasure tower is an expression of the state of Buddhahood that lies dormant within each of us. It teaches us the infinite nobility of life.

Saito: That is what the Daishonin meant when he wrote to a lay follower, Abutsu-bo: "Abutsu-bo is therefore the treasure tower itself, and the treasure tower is Abutsu-bo himself. No other knowledge is purposeful" (WND, 299).

Ikeda: In response to Abutsu-bo's question about the treasure tower, the Daishonin declares definitively, "Your very life is the treasure tower." We can almost hear the Daishonin's warm, compassionate voice.

Endo: In "The Emergence of the Treasure Tower," responding to the wish of those gathered at Eagle Peak, the Buddha uses his supernatural powers to lift them into the air. Here, too, we can sense the Buddha's compassion.

Ikeda: The Buddha does not look down on living beings from on high. He lifts them up to the same level as himself. He teaches them that they are all equally treasure towers worthy of supreme respect. This is the philosophy of the Lotus Sutra and Nichiren Daishonin's spirit. It is true humanism.

The Ceremony in the Air described in "The Emergence of the Treasure Tower" also expresses the Buddha's compassion to strive with all his might to communicate his state of enlightenment to all sentient beings.

Saito: When the beings gathered to hear the Lotus Sutra are lifted into the air, you could say they break free from the fetters of the earth of ignorance and rise into the free and unobstructed skies of the Dharma nature.

Suda: We find such expressions in the Daishonin's writings as "the sky of the true aspect of all phenomena and the reality of all things" and "the sky of the essential nature of phenomena" (WND, 1030). I think we can see at least part of the significance of the concepts of sky, space or air—as in the Ceremony in the Air—in these expressions.

Ikeda: The Daishonin also said, "Hence, the 'air' represents the Land of Eternally Tranquil Light" (GZ, 742). The Ceremony in the Air represents the vast and unbounded state of the Buddha, the state of enlightenment. This realm of ultimate reality and truth transcends both time and space.

Spatially, it extends infinitely throughout the universe. In "The Emergence of the Treasure Tower," where the Ceremony in the Air begins, we see the event known as "the three transformations of the land," during which Shakyamuni purifies and transforms the *saha* and countless other worlds into a vast, unbounded Buddha land. Also, in "Supernatural Powers of the Thus Come One" and "Entrustment," where the Ceremony in the Air concludes, the Buddha, using one of his ten mystic or supernatural powers, reveals that all of the lands in the ten directions (the eight points of the compass, as well as above and below) are one unobstructed Buddha land.

Temporally, this realm of ultimate reality is eternal. The Ceremony in the Air begins with Many Treasures Buddha of the past and Shakyamuni of the present seated side by side in the treasure tower. Then Bodhisattva Superior Practices, a Buddha of the future, is called forth, and the teaching is entrusted to him. The past, present and future are all encompassed by this ceremony.

Indeed, there is perhaps no more fitting way to express the eternal and limitless state of Buddhahood than by using the Ceremony in the Air—a setting that breaks all boundaries of time and space.

Endo: And the Lotus Sutra expressed this state in a symbolic and visual fashion that makes it easy for ordinary people to understand.

Ikeda: Since the Ceremony in the Air transcends any given time or place, it conversely belongs to any time, era or place. Here, however, we must consider not only the significance of the Ceremony in the Air but the meaning of the Lotus Sutra's entire progression in terms of three assemblies in two places.

Suda: I believe the relationship between the two assemblies on Eagle Peak and the Ceremony in the Air has profound significance in terms of our Buddhist view of life.

Ikeda: Yes, the progression from the assembly at Eagle Peak to the Ceremony in the Air and then back to Eagle Peak parallels the movement from reality to the state of enlightenment and then back to reality. Or, more accurately, it flows from reality prior to enlightenment to the state of enlightenment and then to reality after enlightenment.

We must strive to cut ourselves free from the chains of time and space, earthly desires and the sufferings of birth and death that keep us confined to the earth of reality and to reach the air or lofty skies of enlightenment from which we can gaze serenely upon all things. From that magnificent height, we can see all our sufferings, problems and passing emotions as nothing but the most insignificant and fleeting events unfolding in a world as tiny as a piece of flotsam in the vast ocean.

Nichiren Daishonin writes: "Suffer what there is to suffer, enjoy what there is to enjoy. Regard both suffering and joy as facts of life, and continue chanting Nam-myoho-renge-kyo, no matter what happens. How could this be anything other than the boundless joy of the Law?" (WND, 681).

This is the perspective from the air—the perspective of Buddhism and the perspective of faith. Chanting Nam-myoho-renge-kyo is the practice that enables us to achieve this perspective.

The Daishonin also declares: "The 'place' where Nichiren and his followers chant Nam-myoho-renge-kyo and dwell in faith corresponds to the passage 'reside in the air.' In other words, they reside in the Ceremony in the Air" (GZ, 740).

By exerting ourselves in faith, chanting daimoku and performing gongyo before the Gohonzon, we immediately become a part of the assembly in the air. Nothing could be more wonderful than this. Mr. Toda often said, "In the daily lives of us ordinary people, there is no place as sacred as the place where we practice gongyo and chant daimoku."

To "rise into the air" means to elevate our state of life through our determined and unwavering faith. This is the significance of the sutra's progression from the first assembly on Eagle Peak to the Ceremony in the Air.

Saito: Then the subsequent progression from the Ceremony in the Air back to Eagle Peak represents returning to the reality of daily life and society and facing its challenges based on the life force of Buddhahood we have tapped through gongyo and daimoku.

Ikeda: Yes. Daily life equals faith, and faith equals daily life. The Lotus Sutra is never divorced from reality. That is its greatness.

Once we have dwelt in the Ceremony in the Air, the reality of daily life, however contemptible it may have formerly seemed, becomes a means for demonstrating our Buddhahood to others. Sufferings and problems enable us to deepen our faith and, by overcoming them, to show actual proof of the benefit of faith. This is the meaning of the Buddhist principles 'earthly desires are enlightenment' and 'changing poison into medicine.'

The defiled realm of the nine worlds is transformed into the world of Buddhahood. This is what Nichiren Daishonin means when he writes "[T]he nine worlds have the potential for Bud-dhahood" (WND, 539). The progression in the Lotus Sutra from the first assembly on Eagle Peak to the Ceremony in the Air illus-trates this principle. Meanwhile, the progression from the Cere-mony in the Air back to Eagle Peak indicates that "Buddhahood retains the nine worlds" (WND, 539). In other words, when we willingly return from the world of Buddhahood into the nine worlds to courageously guide others to enlightenment, the impure land of the nine worlds is illuminated by the world of Buddha-hood and transformed into the Land of Eternally Tranquil Light, a shining Buddha land. Here we see the principle that 'the impure land is the Land of Eternally Tranquil Light' at work.

At that moment, this world of impermanence, suffering, non-self and impurity becomes a world of eternity, happiness, true self and purity. The Daishonin writes, "Illuminated by the light of the five characters of the Mystic Law, they display the dignified attributes that they inherently possess" (WND, 832). All of the nine worlds, as symbolized by the various beings who gather to hear the Lotus Sutra in the "Introduction" chapter, are illuminated by the Mystic Law. Ordinary people, just as they are, can reveal their true and most supremely noble selves and in turn illuminate society with their radiance.

From real life to the Ceremony in the Air and then back to real life—this continuous back-and-forth process is the path of human revolution, the path of transforming our state of life from one motivated by the 'lesser self' to one inspired by the 'greater self.' In life, we must not permit ourselves to be totally absorbed with only immediate realities. We must have ideals and strive to achieve them, thereby transcending present realities. On the other hand, we must not allow ourselves to become estranged from reality. We can change nothing unless our feet are firmly planted on the ground.

Many people and also many religions tend to choose one of two paths. Either they compromise with the realities of society and lose their identity or, seeking to evade these realities, they remove themselves entirely from society and try to create their own separate world. Both approaches are mistaken.

The essence of the Lotus Sutra lies in neither of those approaches. The Lotus Sutra teaches a way of life in which we gaze serenely at reality from an elevated state of life—high in the air, as it were —and yet, at the same time, actively involve ourselves in those realities as reformers. I think this overall structure of the three assemblies in two places is brilliantly expressed in the Lotus Sutra's characteristic as a reformist religious teaching.

Saito: I agree. The emphasis on reformation is also one of the most distinctive features of Nichiren Daishonin's Buddhism.

Ikeda: Yes. As a matter of fact, the distinction between the Daishonin's Buddhism and Shakyamuni's Buddhism can be explained in terms of the framework of the three assemblies in two places.

Suda: Could you elaborate on that?

Ikeda: Shakyamuni's Buddhism, if anything, emphasizes the movement from Eagle Peak to the Ceremony in the Air—in other words, leaving this world in search of the realm of the Buddha's wisdom. The goal of this search, in a nutshell, is Nam-myoho-renge-kyo, the teaching implicit in the depths of the "Life Span" chapter expounded during the Ceremony in the Air.

In contrast, the Daishonin's Buddhism emphasizes the progression from the depths of "Life Span" expounded during the Ceremony in the Air back to Eagle Peak—that is, from Nam-myoho-renge-kyo back to real life. It is a Buddhism that aims for the transformation of reality, and the practice of this Buddhism is to undertake compassionate actions among the people.

Saito: Perhaps we could say that of the two types of bodhisattva practices, 'seeking enlightenment above' and 'guiding sentient beings below,' Shakyamuni's Buddhism emphasizes the former while the Daishonin's Buddhism emphasizes the latter.

Ikeda: That's precisely it. Of course, tireless efforts to seek enlightenment above are essential in any efforts to guide sentient beings below. Another way of describing the difference in emphasis is to say that the dynamic of Shakyamuni's Buddhism is 'from the cause to the effect,' while that of the Daishonin's Buddhism is 'from the effect to the cause.'

This is a somewhat difficult subject, but basically the principle 'from the cause to the effect' refers to people of the nine worlds (the cause) practicing in order to attain Buddhahood (the effect). In contrast, the principle 'from the effect to the cause' indicates people who, based on the state of Buddhahood (the effect) they have attained instantly through chanting daimoku to the Gohonzon, pursue and challenge the reality of the nine worlds (the cause) in daily life.

You might say Shakyamuni's Buddhism is like climbing a mountain, starting at the foot and heading for the summit. During the ascent, we are given explanations of how wonderful the peak is, but we ourselves cannot appreciate or comprehend it. Nor is there any guarantee we will eventually reach the top. We may get lost or meet with an accident on the way. In contrast, the Daishonin's Buddhism reveals the way to the direct and immediate attainment of enlightenment, so in an instant we find ourselves standing on the mountain peak. There, we personally savor the marvelous view with our whole beings and, out of our desire to share that joy with others, we descend and go out into society.

Saito: In the Lotus Sutra, propagation of the teachings after the Buddha's death is entrusted not to the bodhisattvas of the theoretical teaching who climbed the mountain but to the Bodhisattvas of the Earth who already stood on the peak (evidencing proof of their Buddhahood) and have returned to work in the realm of actual society.

Ikeda: In terms of faith and practice, our daily practice of gongyo and daimoku may be viewed in a general sense as a practice that leads us from the nine worlds to Buddhahood. As such, it could be called a practice that leads from the cause to the effect. On a more profound level, however, our practice of gongyo and daimoku itself directly connects us to the state of Buddhahood. This daily practice serves as the starting point for activities that lead from the effect to the cause — in other words, activities that spread the wisdom and compassion of the Mystic Law into daily life.

The faith of those who chant daimoku with devotion to the Gohonzon simultaneously encompasses the two directions — from the cause to the effect and from the effect to the cause. This is what sets the Buddhism of Nichiren Daishonin in a class of its own.

Saito: Nam (dedicating our lives) of Nam-myoho-renge-kyo means both to return to and to take action based on Myoho-renge-kyo, the Mystic Law. Nam-myoho-renge-kyo, therefore, encompasses the two directions in this activity.

Both directions, I feel, are found in the state of the Buddha's enlightenment itself. Unless both directions are present, it could not be called true enlightenment. This may be one reason why the Lotus Sutra strives to communicate the totality of the Buddha's enlightenment through the format of the 'three assemblies in two places.'

Ikeda: Let's make that a topic for further investigation. In any case, the Lotus Sutra is an amazing scripture. It tells us how profound and unfathomable the Buddha's wisdom is—that enlightenment is not something that can be grasped as an intellectual concept, that it cannot be fully expressed in words. While praising the Buddha's wisdom in this way, it also declares that the purpose of the Buddha's appearance in the world is to make this ineffable wisdom accessible to all beings and enable them to attain enlightenment. The Lotus Sutra also emphasizes that it is expounded for this reason and that all who hear it will attain Buddhahood without fail. The sutra states again and again that, even after the Buddha's death, a person who hears the Lotus Sutra and commits so much as a single phrase or verse to memory will, without fail, attain Buddhahood.

Just to hear it is sufficient to attain enlightenment—this is how the blessings and benefits of the Lotus Sutra are lauded. However, no explicit mention is made of the actual details of that enlightenment. Scriptures that praise themselves with such untiring enthusiasm are rare. This is another amazing facet of the Lotus Sutra, and one of its secrets. The Ceremony in the Air and the three assemblies in two places are keys to unlocking the secret of the Lotus Sutra.

Endo: That the three assemblies in two places expresses the totality of the Buddha's enlightenment can also be seen in the term *Thus Come One,* one of the ten honorable titles of the Buddha. In Mahayana Buddhism, the Thus Come One is defined as "one who has come from the world of truth." That is, the Buddha appears from the world of enlightenment, the world of truth, and, as a person who embodies wisdom and compassion, leads other beings to enlightenment.

Ikeda: A Buddha is a person of action and fighting spirit. A Buddha is not content to remain comfortably in the realm of enlightenment. A Buddha or Thus Come One continues to struggle on the "earth" of the nine worlds for the sake of others, for the happiness of all. The Daishonin writes: "The words of a wise man of old also teach that 'you should base your mind on the ninth consciousness, and carry out your practice in the six consciousnesses.'[3] How reasonable it is too!" (WND, 458). Basing the mind on the ninth consciousness corresponds to "residing in the Ceremony in the Air" or dwelling in faith, while carrying out practice in the six consciousnesses means never allowing ourselves to become separated from reality.

Suda: This passage, then, teaches us the significance of the three assemblies in two places, especially the movement from the Ceremony in the Air back to the second assembly on Eagle Peak. We can also say it reveals the spirit of the Thus Come One, who emerges from the realm of truth.

Saito: In the second assembly on Eagle Peak, Bodhisattva Medicine King, Bodhisattva Mystic Sound, Bodhisattva Perceiver of the World's Sounds, Bodhisattva Universal Wisdom and others take center stage. All of these bodhisattvas essentially practice the way of the Thus Come One and, while displaying their respective powers and capabilities, they assist in propagating the Lotus Sutra after Shakyamuni's death.

Ikeda: After the Ceremony in the Air, the functions of these bodhisattvas in the real world are explained in all their splendid variety. This is very significant.

Endo: They carry out their activities as expressions of wisdom and joy based on the life state of Buddhahood.

Ikeda: Yes, that's right. The SGI's global movement to promote peace, culture and education based on Buddhism also follows this same formula. The vibrant spirituality and dynamic, creative cultural force of the Lotus Sutra are revealed in its capacity to manifest the vibrant pulse of the eternity of life in society and, in doing so, transform the world.

Suda: In Japan, many people view Buddhism as a cloistered religious world, but that is certainly not true.

Ikeda: That popular image of Buddhism has been entirely the fault of the leaders of Japan's major Buddhist schools. Buddhism does not exist apart from society. Buddhism manifests itself in society, and society reflects Buddhism. With this conviction, as a Buddhist and private citizen, I have met and conducted dialogues with many world leaders of various fields and, though my contributions might be small, I have searched with them for answers to the problems that confront all humanity.

The message and wisdom of Buddhism must always be carried dynamically into society and the world. That is what the Daishonin's Buddhism is all about. A religion that remains cloistered in the religious realm, closed off from the rest of the world, is in effect committing suicide. According to the Daishonin, "the Lotus Sutra explains that in the end secular matters are the entirety of Buddhism" (WND, 1126).

THE THREE ASSEMBLIES IN TWO PLACES DESCRIBES THE TOTALITY OF LIFE

Endo: Since the Ceremony in the Air corresponds to a realm of eternity that spans past, present and future, the Shakyamuni who preaches to the assembly in the air must also be an eternally existing entity that transcends the historical personage.

Ikeda: The Ceremony in the Air takes place in a realm transcending time and space, so of course the Buddha preaching in that realm is not the historical Shakyamuni but an "eternal Buddha." This is presented in detail in the "Life Span" chapter as the enlightenment Shakyamuni attained in the remote past. The setting for this revelation, however, is introduced in "The Emergence of the Treasure Tower" chapter.

At the same time, that eternal Buddha embodies the truth of the Law to which Shakyamuni became enlightened—in other words, the truth that "the treasure tower adorned with the seven kinds of treasures" (WND, 299) exists in our lives. When the members of the assembly are lifted into the sky, they are brought into this realm of truth; that is, all living beings are eternal Buddhas.

The Daishonin writes: "Shakyamuni Buddha, the lord of teachings, who said numberless major world system dust particle kalpas ago, 'I am the only person [who can rescue and protect others,]' refers to living beings like ourselves" (WND, 36).

The Ceremony in the Air is a realm in which all living beings of the Ten Worlds are equal, and where there is no distinction between sentient beings and the Buddha.

Suda: A realm in which ordinary people and the Buddha are not two separate entities—this is the realm of 'the oneness of sentient beings and the Buddha.' In "The True Object of Worship," the Daishonin declares: "The Buddha neither has entered into extinction in the past nor will be born in the future. And the same is true of his disciples" (WND, 366). Those who hear the Buddha's teachings, he says, are one in body with the Buddha.

Saito: Mr. Toda declared that the life of each individual is one with the life of the universe and with the life of the Buddha. From the perspective that the self is one with the universe and the universe is one with the self, the progression of the three assemblies in two places is a continuous cycle — rising from the earth of reality on Eagle Peak to the Ceremony in the Air that unfolds into the vast universe and then back again to Eagle Peak. It is a drama, if you like, of the interaction of the microcosm and the macrocosm. I can't help feeling that the purpose of the Ceremony in the Air, the progression of three assemblies in two places, is to provide us with the actual experience — not just a conceptual understanding — of the life of the universe.

Ikeda: Yes. The three assemblies in two places expresses the totality of life, the dynamism of life. It demonstrates, for instance, the principle of 'the oneness of body and mind.'

Saito: In the "Orally Transmitted Teachings," the Daishonin states: "The earth represents the phenomenon of the body, while the air represents the phenomenon of the mind. But we should understand that body and mind are not two separate entities" (GZ, 742).

Ikeda: I think we can also say that the three assemblies in two places also expresses the oneness of life and death.

Endo: Yes. The Daishonin goes on to say, "The passage 'all the members of the great assembly are in the air' refers to ourselves in death" (GZ, 742). Consequently, if the Ceremony in the Air represents death, then Eagle Peak represents life.

The three assemblies in two places thus also represents the dynamic movement from life to death and to life again. It reveals the true aspect of life and death as one inseparable phenomena.

Ikeda: That's true. I think we can also discuss this from the perspective of the Daishonin's words in "The Heritage of the Ultimate Law of Life": "The ultimate law of life and death as transmitted from the Buddha to all living beings is Myoho-renge-kyo.... *Myo* represents death, and *ho*, life" (WND, 216).

Saito: Discussed from this perspective, the air—the aspect of death —is equivalent to *myo*, and Eagle Peak—the aspect of life—is equivalent to *ho*.

Ikeda: Yes. The air is an eternally unchanging realm, symbolizing the world of the Buddha's enlightenment. It is equivalent to the *myo*, or "mystic," of *myoho*, the Mystic Law, because it is an unfathomable realm, a realm beyond the conceptualization of us ordinary people. In contrast, Eagle Peak, as a real place, corresponds to *ho*, which means not only the "Law" but "phenomena." It represents the aspect of life.

Myo (death) and *ho* (life) are inseparable. In addition, the truth of the oneness of life and death throughout the universe is also expressed by the two Buddhas seated together in the Ceremony in the Air.

Suda: The Daishonin writes, "Shakyamuni and Many Treasures, the two Buddhas, are also the two phases of life and death" (WND, 216). The Buddha of the present, Shakyamuni, represents life, and the Buddha of the past, Many Treasures, represents death.

Ikeda: Life and death are indeed the most fundamental issues we face. In a sense, the Lotus Sutra itself elucidates the two phases of life and death. The "Introduction" chapter begins with the word *this* of the expression "This is what I heard" (LS1, 3), and the last chapter of the sutra, "Bodhisattva Universal Wisdom," ends with the word *departed*—"they bowed in obeisance and departed" (LS28, 324). Based on this, the Daishonin says, "The two characters *nyo* (this) and *ko* (departed) represent the two phases of life and death" (GZ, 782).

The deeper we look into the three assemblies in two places, the more we will learn; it is an inexhaustible fountain of wisdom and insights. I'm sure we'll have an opportunity to pursue this further later.

The important thing is that we act out the three assemblies in two places in our daily lives. Nichiren Daishonin used the Ceremony in the Air to express his own enlightenment in the form of the Gohonzon. We who embrace the Gohonzon manifest the dynamism of the Lotus Sutra directly in our lives.

It is impossible to calculate the number of people who have studied and read and recited the Lotus Sutra through the ages. We of the SGI should take great pride in living the true essence of the sutra.

As we practice the Mystic Law, each moment of our lives is linked directly to the Ceremony in the Air, the world of ultimate truth, and we can savor the realm of eternity. Light, breezes, music and the fragrance of benefit and good fortune flow into our lives from the Mystic Law's infinite universe and gently fold us in their embrace.

When we devote our lives to the propagation of the Mystic Law, the present moment for us is always one with eternity. Eternity and the present moment meet, interact and reverberate in harmonious unity in our daily lives. Our lives are a continuous stream of joy—a manifestation of eternity in the present moment. Therefore, to a person of faith, a single moment is not just a single moment, a day is not just a day. Each moment, each day, has an eternity of value packed into it. The more time passes, the more each moment, each day, shines with golden light.

The Lotus Sutra teaches us this unsurpassed way of living. Toward that end, what were the first words spoken by Shakyamuni in the sutra? We will discuss this in the next chapter, where we will begin to explore "Expedient Means."

NOTES

1. Rajagriha: Present-day Rajgir in India.

2. Translated from Japanese: *Toda Josei Zenshu* (The Collected Works of Josei Toda) (Tokyo: Seikyo Shimbunsha, 1986), vol. 6, pp. 591–92.

3. Of the nine consciousnesses, the first five relate to the five senses of sight, hearing, smell, taste and touch. The sixth consciousness integrates the perceptions of the first five and renders them into a coherent image. The ninth, or *amala*-consciousness, is the fundamental purifying force, free from all karmic impurity; that is, the Buddha nature.

PART THREE

"Expedient Means" Chapter

6 "Expedient Means": The Art of Skillful Human Education

Ikeda: Our world is in chaos. Both society and the realm of ideas are in disarray. Sensible people are now thinking seriously about where the world is headed. Many feel a strong sense of crisis that, if we continue as we are, humanity and society will eventually collapse like a house without pillars. They are searching for a clear guideline as to how human beings should live. Many are starting to think earnestly about religion—not as something far removed from daily concerns but as something very close to home. They question what attitude to take toward religion, how to regard and approach it. In this context, exploring religion in the twenty-first century through this Lotus Sutra discussion has great significance.

Saito: We will at last begin discussing "Expedient Means." We are all familiar with this chapter, of course, because we recite a portion from it during morning and evening gongyo.

Of the twenty-eight Lotus Sutra chapters, "Expedient Means" is the third longest after the "Simile and Parable" and "Parable of the Phantom City" chapters. The portion we recite during gongyo —namely, from the chapter opening to the enunciation of the ten factors of life, which represent the true entity of all phenomena—is only one-twentieth of the whole "Expedient Means" chapter. This, explains the twenty-sixth high priest, Nichikan, is because it includes the chapter's most important teaching, and there is no need to recite the remaining portion.

Ikeda: Yes. Doctrinally speaking, "Expedient Means" and "Life Span" are the two pivotal Lotus Sutra chapters. Understanding "Expedient Means" in particular is indispensable to grasping the significance of Nam-myoho-renge-kyo.

OVERVIEW OF "EXPEDIENT MEANS"

Suda: In the "Introduction" chapter, Shakyamuni enters a deep meditation—"the samadhi of the place of immeasurable meanings" (LS1, 5). In "Expedient Means," he arises from his meditation, or *samadhi*, and suddenly turns to Shariputra and says: "The wisdom of the Buddhas is infinitely profound and immeasurable. The door to this wisdom is difficult to understand and difficult to enter" (LS2, 23). He then begins to describe the wondrousness of this Buddha wisdom.

Ikeda: These are the first words Shakyamuni actually speaks in the Lotus Sutra. This first utterance has a special significance. It is a dramatic expression of the fact that the Lotus Sutra teaches the Buddha's wisdom just as it is, according to the Buddha's own mind.

The profound and immeasurable Buddha wisdom is comprehensible only to Buddhas. That is why Shakyamuni begins by praising the Buddha wisdom on his own initiative and not in response to any question. Indeed, his use of the unsolicited and spontaneous teaching format from the outset of this chapter underscores how profound and unfathomable the Buddha wisdom is—so much so that none of the assembly could have even conceived a question about it.

Endo: Because the Law to which the Buddha has awakened is "the rarest and most difficult-to-understand Law" (LS2, 24), only Buddhas can comprehend it.

Ikeda: Yes. Shakyamuni declares, "The true entity of all phenomena can only be understood and shared between Buddhas" (LS2,

24). It's as if he said to Shariputra, who was lauded as "foremost in wisdom": "There's no way you and the others can comprehend this." This naturally must have surprised everyone present.

Suda: Shariputra's heart probably very nearly stopped!

Saito: Shariputra demonstrated unrivaled excellence among those of the two vehicles—Learning and Realization (the voice-hearers and *pratyekabuddhas*). Both he and others clearly recognized his status as the wisest and most learned of Shakyamuni's disciples. When Shakyamuni declares that not even Shariputra with all his wisdom can comprehend the Buddha wisdom, the superiority and wonder of the Buddha wisdom is further emphasized.

Endo: This is great theater!

Ikeda: I agree. The question, however, is what constitutes this Buddha wisdom.

Endo: In "Expedient Means," the Law all Buddhas have attained is expressed as "the true entity of all phenomena." The Great Teacher T'ien-t'ai of China developed this into the doctrine of 'three thousand realms in a single moment of life,' and Nichiren Daishonin defined it as Nam-myoho-renge-kyo.

Ikeda: Accordingly, the praise for the Buddha wisdom at the beginning of "Expedient Means" is, from the viewpoint of the Daishonin's Buddhism, praise for Nam-myoho-renge-kyo. This is our prime reason for reciting this passage during gongyo. Why then is this chapter, in which the true wisdom of the Buddhas—namely, the Mystic Law—begins to be elucidated, called "Expedient Means"?

Endo: You mean, why isn't it called the "Wisdom of the Buddhas" or the "Truth" chapter? This question strikes at the very core of "Expedient Means."

Suda: To consider this more fully, it might be best to follow the events that unfold a little further into "Expedient Means." In response to Shakyamuni's earnest praise of the Buddha wisdom, Shariputra, speaking for the entire assembly, begs Shakyamuni to expound the true teachings of the Buddhas. Shariputra requests this three times. Finally, after the third time, Shakyamuni accedes and begins to preach.

Endo: At that crucial moment, some five thousand arrogant monks, nuns, laymen and laywomen leave the assembly. Shakyamuni makes no move to stop them; he allows them to leave in silence.

Ikeda: Much should be said about these five thousand arrogant believers, but one lesson is clear—the arrogant depart at the most decisive moment. Shakyamuni declares firmly: "Shariputra, it is well that these persons of overbearing arrogance have withdrawn. Now listen carefully and I will preach for you" (LS2, 30).

He then reveals to Shariputra that the "one great reason" Buddhas appear in the world is to open the door to the Buddha wisdom for all people, to show it to them, to cause them to awaken to it and gain entry to it.

"Expedient Means" reads:

> The Buddhas, the World-Honored Ones, appear in the world for one great reason alone....
> The Buddhas, the World-Honored Ones, wish to open the door of Buddha wisdom to all living beings, to allow them to attain purity. That is why they appear in the world. They wish to show the Buddha wisdom to living beings, and therefore they appear in the world. They wish to cause living beings to awaken to the Buddha wisdom, and therefore they appear in the world. They wish to induce living beings to enter the path of Buddha wisdom, and therefore they appear in the world. (LS2, 31)

Suda: Yes, Shakyamuni says: "The Buddhas, the World-Honored Ones, appear in the world for one great reason alone" (LS2, 31). That one great reason is revealed as the four aspects of the Buddha's wisdom—to open, to show, to awaken and to help enter.

Ikeda: That the Buddha seeks to open the door of Buddha wisdom [the state of Buddhahood] to living beings means that living beings already inherently possess the Buddha wisdom. The reason they possess the Buddha wisdom is that they are essentially Buddhas. Shakyamuni's words are in fact a great declaration that all living beings are worthy of supreme respect.

Endo: The Buddha then reveals that the three vehicles—Learning, Realization and Bodhisattva—are no more than expedient means, while the one supreme vehicle of Buddhahood offers the only true way to enlightenment.

The term *vehicle* refers to the Buddha's teaching, which carries people from ignorance and confusion to enlightenment. The three vehicles carry people toward the goals of Learning, Realization and Bodhisattva, respectively.

Shakyamuni declares, however, that there are not three separate teachings but only one—one single vehicle. Because it is the teaching for attaining Buddhahood, it is also known as the one Buddha vehicle.

Ikeda: To his followers, it seemed as if Shakyamuni had set forth three separate teachings, but to the Buddha there is only one Buddha vehicle and no other. The one Buddha vehicle is a teaching that enables all people to attain Buddhahood; it is endowed with the function of opening and revealing the Buddha wisdom and awakening and guiding people to the realm of Buddhahood.

Suda: The three vehicles are expedient means to lead people to the one Buddha vehicle, which is the Buddha's true intent and purpose.

In "Expedient Means," Shakyamuni explains the true function of the three vehicles and reveals the truth of the one Buddha vehicle. This is referred to as 'the replacement of the three vehicles with the one vehicle.' He then cites examples of how he as well as the Buddhas of the past, present and future throughout the ten directions have resorted to expedient means to help people attain the one Buddha vehicle.

Many important teachings are preached by Buddhas of each period, but let us leave this for another discussion. In essence, Shakyamuni tells us that the true intent behind the teachings of all Buddhas, including himself, is to expound the one Buddha vehicle.

The clarification of the three vehicles as expedient means and the one Buddha vehicle as the sole means to attain Buddha wisdom does not end with "Expedient Means"; it continues on through "Prophecies Conferred on Learners and Adepts," the ninth chapter. It is a major theme of the first half—or theoretical teaching—of the Lotus Sutra.

THE LOTUS SUTRA IS THE "SECRET AND MYSTIC EXPEDIENT"

Ikeda: We can see that expedient means form an important premise in the concept of 'the replacement of the three vehicles with the one vehicle,' which is central to the "Expedient Means" chapter. In fact, the term *expedient means* is a key not only in clarifying the one Buddha vehicle and refuting the three vehicles in the Lotus Sutra's theoretical teaching but also in revealing Shakyamuni's original enlightenment numberless major world system dust particle kalpas ago in the "Life Span" chapter of the essential teaching. With this revelation, it becomes clear that Shakyamuni's attainment of enlightenment in India was an expedient means, while in truth he attained enlightenment in the inconceivably distant past. This concept is called 'opening the near and revealing the distant.'

Saito: Viewed from the Lotus Sutra as a whole, we could even say that the subject of expedient means is given far greater weight than the 'replacement of the three vehicles with the one vehicle' itself.

Endo: In the Sanskrit text, the expression "expedient means" of the "Expedient Means" chapter is *upaya kaushalya. Upaya* means "approach" or "means of approach," and *kaushalya* means "excellent" or "skillful."

Ikeda: In other words, expedient means are educational techniques for leading people to Buddhahood. The spirit of the Lotus Sutra is to bring each human being's enormous potential into fullest flower, and for that the Buddha uses expedient means. Expedient means are methods for educating people in the broadest sense.

In fact, the first Soka Gakkai president, Tsunesaburo Makiguchi, who was also an educator, outlined his own educational method in terms of opening, showing, awakening and guiding. What Mr. Makiguchi did was to incorporate the Buddha's method for leading people to enlightenment into his own educational method.

Endo: I didn't know that. But it certainly makes sense. Mr. Makiguchi's educational system always aimed to maximize each student's potential. He maintained: "Education is not selling bits of knowledge or pouring information into a student's head. True education is awakening in the student a method for acquiring knowledge through his or her own powers, providing the student with the key to unlock the storehouse of knowledge."[1]

Ikeda: Mr. Makiguchi asserted that vague educational goals were the underlying problem with education in his day, and he declared, "The purpose of education is to make children happy." At a time when many regarded education's purpose as developing people who would be "useful to the nation," Mr. Makiguchi's educational view, which placed the highest importance on children and on the individual, was revolutionary indeed. The main objective of value-creating education at its inception, therefore, was to help each individual develop the power to achieve personal happiness.

Mr. Makiguchi also insisted that education requires special techniques, just as do the fields of medicine, agriculture and engineering. Merely pouring knowledge into the empty vessel of the student or hoping that some vague character-building will take place through the teacher's natural influence would not suffice as tools for proper education, he asserted. Techniques—in other words, expedient means—were needed.

Based on that idea, Mr. Makiguchi categorized teachers into three levels: those lacking technique; those possessing technique; and those possessing art. Mr. Makiguchi gave his heart and soul to searching for the best way to contribute to children's happiness— how to bring out their abilities, their capacity for value-creation, so they could lead happy lives; how to open the door to their individual potential—to help show them, awaken them and gain them entry to it. Mr. Makiguchi's system of pedagogy was not just an armchair theory but an approach born out of actual practice in the classroom, his love for children and his compassionate wish to help them.

Saito: That love and compassion gave rise to a great body of wisdom. And that, I think, is the very life of value-creating education. I am reminded of the dilemma facing Shakyamuni after he attained enlightenment. He is said to have been troubled over whether he should teach his enlightenment to others. In "Expedient Means," Shakyamuni describes his reasons for hesitating:

> Shariputra, you should understand
> that I view things through the Buddha eye,
> I see the living beings in the six paths,
> how poor and distressed they are, without merit
>   or wisdom,
> how they enter the perilous road of birth and death,
> their sufferings continuing with never a break,

how deeply they are attached to the five desires,
like a yak enamored of its tail,
blinding themselves with greed and infatuation,
their vision so impaired they can see nothing.
They do not seek the Buddha, with his great might,
or the Law that can end their sufferings,
but enter deeply into erroneous views,
hoping to shed suffering through greater suffering.
For the sake of these living beings
I summon up a mind of great compassion. (LS2, 42)

Suda: Shakyamuni was also aware of how hard people were to save:

With persons such as this,
what can I say, how can I save them?...
Immediately I thought to myself
that if I merely praised the Buddha vehicle,
then the living beings, sunk in their suffering,
would be incapable of believing in this Law.
And because they rejected the Law and failed
   to believe in it,
they would fall into the three evil paths.
It would be better if I did not preach the Law
but quickly entered into nirvana.
Then my thoughts turned to the Buddhas of the past
and the power of expedient means they had employed,
and I thought that the way I had now attained
should likewise be preached as three vehicles. (LS2, 42–43)

Saito: Then the Buddhas of the ten directions encourage Shakyamuni:

"But following the example of all other Buddhas,
you will employ the power of expedient means." (LS2, 43)

When Shakyamuni hears this, he rejoices and cries, "Hail to the Buddhas!" and then thinks to himself:

> I have come into this impure and evil world,
> and as these Buddhas have preached,
> I too must follow that example in my actions. (LS2, 44)

Ikeda: Shakyamuni's hesitation derived from his profound compassion. To have compassion means to feel others' sufferings as one's own. Because the Buddha is filled with the desire to save others, he agonizes over how to achieve this. Such compassion gives rise to wisdom. This is the power of expedient means and the art of human education. In a certain sense, therefore, a Buddha is someone who is always thinking and agonizing over how to develop others' ability to achieve happiness as well as over how to fulfill his or her own mission.

Saito: The "Life Span" section we recite during gongyo concludes:

> At all times I think to myself:
> How can I cause living beings
> to gain entry into the unsurpassed way
> and quickly acquire the body of a Buddha? (LS16, 232)

By asking himself "How?" the Buddha ponders which means or method would best achieve this aspiration. This passage, too, highlights his compassion to continuously think about how to lead people to happiness.

Ikeda: In "Expedient Means," Shakyamuni says, "I have through various causes and various similes widely expounded my teachings" (LS2, 24). Depending on his audience, the Buddha employs different causes and different similes to lead people to the right path. This Buddha ability is called 'the power of expedient means.'

It is the ability to know precisely what to teach each individual at any given moment.

In other words, it is the ability to perceive each individual's precise state of being and the wisdom to select the most appropriate teaching for that person. It is also the power of compassion that seeks to nurture all people so that they may attain Buddhahood. The source of all these abilities and powers is the profound and immeasurable Buddha wisdom.

Endo: T'ien-t'ai called that essential Buddha wisdom "true wisdom," and he termed the power of expedient means arising from it "provisional wisdom." Shakyamuni praises these two kinds of wisdom—the true and the provisional—at the opening of "Expedient Means."

Suda: Translated into Mr. Makiguchi's terminology, the "power of expedient means" corresponds to art beyond mere technique; more specifically, it corresponds to the highest art of human education.

Saito: Let us now look at the different kinds of expedient means in Buddhism. In *Words and Phrases of the Lotus Sutra,* T'ien-t'ai identifies three types: 'functional-teaching expedients,' 'truth-gateway expedients,' and the 'secret and mystic expedient.' Of the three, says T'ien-t'ai, the last is the expedient means of the "Expedient Means" chapter.

Functional-teaching expedients are the various teachings expounded according to people's differing capacities, the function of these teachings being to bring appropriate benefit to each person. Truth-gateway expedients are teachings that form a gateway for gaining access to the truth, hence the name.

Neither of these two types, however, are the expedient means of the "Expedient Means" chapter. They are two aspects of the expedient means taught in the provisional teachings expounded before the Lotus Sutra. The functional-teaching expedients represent the aspect of bringing immediate benefit, while the truth-gateway expedients represent the aspect of leading people to truth.

Endo: We could cite Shakyamuni's denunciation of those of the two vehicles, who contented themselves with inferior teachings, as having both these aspects. It was a truth-gateway expedient in that it directed the followers of the two vehicles to the truth, yet it also had the aspect of a functional-teaching expedient in that it awakened them from their self-absorption.

At times the Buddha brings joy to living beings, at times he admonishes them sternly. Is it going too far to say it is like the carrot-and-stick method?

Ikeda: I think that would be doing Shakyamuni a bit of a disservice — though there may be a kernel of truth in your observation!

The Buddha's teaching methods are indeed skillful. Among his honorary titles are "Teacher of Heavenly and Human Beings" and "Trainer of People." The Buddha is a teacher of not only humans but heavenly beings as well, and as a trainer of people, he is skilled at forging harmony among people. These titles derive from the fact that the Buddha leads people unerringly based on the loftiest of goals. The Buddha, then, is a superlative teacher of human education.

To return to our subject, when Shakyamuni declares in "Expedient Means" that he will now preach the Law, "honestly discarding expedient means" (LS2, 44), he is discarding the two types of expedient means we have discussed so far — functional-teaching expedients and truth-gateway expedients. The secret and mystic expedient is another thing altogether. It is not an expedient to be discarded; it is an expedient that represents the truth itself.

Endo: We normally tend to regard an expedient means as a method for arriving at the truth rather than as the ultimate truth itself. This makes it extremely difficult to understand the secret and mystic expedient, which, though termed an expedient, is actually the truth.

Ikeda: Yes, I agree. Mr. Toda, too, racked his brains over how best to explain the doctrine of the secret and mystic expedient in a way all could easily understand.

As mentioned earlier, expedient implies an approach, a method leading to a goal. I think we can conceive of two directions in which Buddhist expedients move. One is from daily reality to a state of enlightenment. This applies to functional-teaching expedients and truth-gateway expedients. The other is from the realm of enlightenment to everyday reality. This direction expresses that enlightenment in terms of the real world. This is the direction of the secret and mystic expedient. Thus, though termed an expedient like the others, the direction in which the secret and mystic expedient functions is completely opposite of the others.

Suda: In that respect, the three types of expedients are similar to the 'three assemblies in two places,' which we discussed earlier, aren't they? The dynamic from Eagle Peak to the Ceremony in the Air is equivalent to functional-teaching and truth-gateway expedients, while the dynamic from the Ceremony in the Air back to Eagle Peak is equivalent to the secret and mystic expedient.

Ikeda: Yes, I think you can say that. The wisdom of the Buddhas is profound and immeasurable. It is the ultimate truth, and it cannot be fully described in words. In "Expedient Means," Shakyamuni calls out:

> Stop, stop, no need to speak!
> My Law is wonderful and difficult to ponder. (LS2, 29)

To try to teach this indescribable and inconceivable truth in words, to give it some form of expression—this can only be called an expedient means. Driven by his profound compassion for living beings, however, the Buddha nevertheless resolved to attempt to expound the inexpressible truth. This is the secret and mystic expedient, an expedient identical to Buddha wisdom.

Endo: T'ien-t'ai described functional-teaching and truth-gateway expedients as expedients outside the body of truth, and the secret and mystic expedient as an expedient identical to the body of truth. In other words, the first two types of expedients stand outside the true Buddha wisdom, while the latter is one and the same as the truth. This restates what you just said.

Ikeda: The secret and mystic expedient is the heart of "Expedient Means," hence the chapter's title. *Secret* of "secret and mystic expedient" (GZ, 714) refers to the fact that it is only known and understood by Buddhas. In other words, only Buddhas know the truth that all living beings are Buddhas.

Though that truth is hidden, under certain external conditions it can be revealed. That unfathomable reality of life is called "mystic." In terms of the Ten Worlds, the world of Buddhahood is hidden in the lives of the people of the nine worlds. Upon contact with the appropriate external conditions, however, it can be manifested within the nine worlds. This wonder is called mystic.

In connection with the secret and mystic expedient, Mr. Toda once said:

> You and I are ordinary people. Yet, at the same time, each of us is theoretically a Buddha. To attain Buddhahood means to know that one is a Buddha. This wondrous fact is secret and hidden; hence, the designation "secret and mystic." Buddhas appear in the *saha* world as ordinary human beings to undergo sufferings [in order to save people]. This is the principle of the secret and mystic expedient.

All of you are Bodhisattvas of the Earth. When you have truly grasped this principle with the very depths of your being, you can understand the "Expedient Means" chapter.[2]

And on another occasion, he said:

> The fact that we are just ordinary common mortals is the secret and mystic expedient; the truth is that we are Buddhas. The Gohonzon is also enshrined in our hearts. The very heart of the Daishonin's Buddhism, therefore, lies in the conviction that the Gohonzon enshrined in our Buddhist altar is identical to our own lives.[3]

We ordinary people are Buddhas, just as we are. This is inconceivable, beyond the scope of our comprehension. Therefore, it is "mystic." Those who don't believe in the Lotus Sutra cannot understand this. Therefore, it is "secret."

Saito: In the "Orally Transmitted Teachings," Nichiren Daishonin explains the significance of the secret and mystic expedient as follows:

> That all living things are in fact the Buddha of the true entity of all phenomena is a wonderful thing, an unfathomable thing! But persons who slander the Law are at present unaware of this fact. Therefore, it is referred to as secret. (GZ, 714)

Ikeda: When we realize that we ourselves are Buddhas, then we understand the secret and mystic expedient. The Daishonin writes: "Nevertheless, even though you chant and believe in Myoho-renge-kyo, if you think the Law is outside yourself, you are embracing not the Mystic Law but an inferior teaching" (WND, 3).

Mystic of "secret and mystic expedient" indicates the wonder, the unfathomable nature of human life. In other words, the nine worlds are all entities of Buddhahood. This is the principle that 'the nine worlds have the potential for Buddhahood.' When one understands this truth, it becomes apparent that Buddhahood does not manifest itself anywhere apart from the nine worlds of ordinary living beings. It only appears within the nine worlds. This is the principle that 'Buddhahood retains the nine worlds.'

If we regard our goal of Buddhahood as "truth" and the nine worlds as "expedient means," then expedient means are identical to truth (the nine worlds have the potential for Buddhahood), while truth is identical to expedient means (Buddhahood retains the nine worlds). This is the meaning of the secret and mystic expedient.

For example, after we have embraced faith in the Gohonzon, the sufferings of the nine worlds are no longer mere sufferings. Instead, they serve to invigorate our faith and strengthen the state of Buddhahood within our lives; they become sufferings in terms of the secret and mystic expedient, in that by triumphing over them, we can show proof of our Buddhahood to others. Suffering becomes a source of motivation—like a megaphone cheering us on to further spiritual growth and achievement.

Endo: The Daishonin writes:

> The five characters of Myoho-renge-kyo represent the ninth consciousness, while the "Expedient Means" chapter presents the levels from the eighth to the first consciousness. The ninth consciousness is the realm of enlightenment, while the levels from the eighth to the first consciousness are the realm of delusion. Since the chapter is titled "Myoho-renge-kyo Hoben-pon" (Lotus Sutra of the Wonderful Law, Expedient Means Chapter), this indicates that delusion and enlightenment are not two different things. This means that of all the

myriad phenomena and the three thousand conditions
or realms, none are not part of the truth of the expedient means of Myoho-renge-kyo. (GZ, 794)

Ikeda: To those who believe in the Daishonin's Buddhism, all phenomena—birth and death, suffering and joy, benefit and loss, all
things and events, all forms and appearances—are manifestations
of the Mystic Law as well as expedient means that lead us to the
Mystic Law. Mr. Toda said, "Both loss and benefit are expedient
means."

Let us look at the example of a person who, before starting to
practice the Daishonin's Buddhism, was afflicted by a problem. As
a result, he or she was probably in the state of Hell. That problem,
however, motivated that person to embrace the Gohonzon. In
such a case, the world of Hell is immediately transformed into
Buddhahood. The particular problem served as a functional-
teaching expedient or a truth-gateway expedient for the individual,
though of the two, I'm more inclined to say it's a truth-gateway
expedient.

Yet even after we embrace faith, we continue to experience
various problems and suffering. We may reach a deadlock and be
unable to break through. But because of our Buddhist practice, any
problem we encounter serves as an opportunity to show actual
proof of the power of faith. Here, we see the secret and mystic
expedient at work.

Problems or difficulties encountered in the course of our efforts
for kosen-rufu, in particular, exemplify the principles that 'the
world of Hell contains the world of the Bodhisattva' and 'the
world of Buddhahood contains the world of Hell.' No problems
or difficulties could be nobler than these. The more we challenge
and triumph over our problems, the stronger Buddhahood grows
within us. In that sense, if our faith is strong, negative factors
immediately transform into positive factors, and loss transforms
into merit. To a person of faith, everything that happens in life
becomes a benefit.

Whatever our circumstances, everything that happens is a vital scene in the drama of our present lifetime in this world—the drama of attaining Buddhahood, which is synonymous with the process of human revolution. Everything is an expedient means (the nine worlds) to reveal the truth (the world of Buddhahood). This is the function of the secret and mystic expedient.

The Daishonin writes: "Suffer what there is to suffer, enjoy what there is to enjoy. Regard both suffering and joy as facts of life, and continue chanting Nam-myoho-renge-kyo, no matter what happens. How could this be anything other than the boundless joy of the Law?" (WND, 681).

Suffering and joy are expedients of the nine worlds. To chant Nam-myoho-renge-kyo is to be in the world of Buddhahood, the realm of the Buddha's true wisdom.

From the vast, elevated state of life we attain through our practice of faith, we gaze serenely upon all sufferings and joys, and at the same time we savor the joy of the Mystic Law. This is what it means to have read the "Expedient Means" chapter with one's entire being.

Saito: I think we can also explore this view of expedient means from the perspective of the eternity of life. In the "Prophecy of Enlightenment for Five Hundred Disciples" chapter, we find the passage:

> Before the multitude they [the sons of the Buddha] seem
>   possessed of the three poisons
> or manifest the signs of heretical views.
> My disciples in this manner
> use expedient means to save living beings. (LS8, 146–47)

This means that even those born as ordinary mortals steeped in the three poisons or deluded by heretical views can lead others in the same condition to enlightenment once they awaken to the Mystic Law. Their circumstances then become expedient means for guiding others.

Ikeda: Yes. This is something we come to appreciate once we awaken to our fundamental mission to practice the eternal Law of Myoho-renge-kyo ourselves and at the same time teach it to others. This is the profoundest view of human life.

We who uphold the Mystic Law are fundamentally noble Bodhisattvas of the Earth. We are comrades who pledged together at the Ceremony in the Air to carry out kosen-rufu. Mr. Toda often called upon members to "recall" that fact.

At the same time, we are ordinary human beings. We appear in this form and experience various sufferings all at our own seeking. This is the principle that practitioners voluntarily choose to be born in adverse circumstances so that they may help others. Being born as a common mortal is the karma (expedient means) we have taken on so that we may demonstrate the power of the Mystic Law (truth). It is, therefore, inconceivable that we cannot overcome any problem that confronts us. We are all playing a leading role, having taken our place in this trouble-filled *saha* world to act out the drama of kosen-rufu.

Endo: At times we forget we are playing a role [that it is all an expedient means]; we give ourselves up so completely to being the anguished and tormented hero that we end up drowning in pain and suffering. But we mustn't let that happen.

Saito: Let's pursue our discussion on the secret and mystic expedient a little further. Consider the relationship between expedient means and the ultimate truth in terms of the provisional teachings (the pre-Lotus Sutra teachings) and the true teaching (the Lotus Sutra). The provisional teachings (expedient means) have one meaning before embracing faith in Nam-myoho-renge-kyo and a different meaning after. Before embracing faith, Nichiren Daishonin states, they are "the provisional teachings outside the body of truth," and after, they become "the provisional teachings within the body of truth."

He says:

> But in the end, persons who slander the Law and fail
> to have faith in it are followers of provisional teachings
> outside the body of the truth, the teachings represented
> by the two types of expedient means known as 'func-
> tional-teaching expedients' and 'truth-gateway expe-
> dients.'... Now Nichiren and his followers, who recite
> Nam-myoho-renge-kyo, are observers of the 'secret and
> mystic expedient,' a teaching that is within the body of
> truth. (GZ, 714)

Once one enters the realm of the wisdom of the Lotus Sutra
(the true teaching), all other extemporaneous teachings expounded by the Buddha up to that point (the provisional teachings)
become provisional teachings within the body of truth, and each
is given its proper place and role within the whole. Thus, without
being discarded, the provisional teachings become partial truths
that bear testimony to the Lotus Sutra's ultimate truth.

Ikeda: Yes. In terms of the earlier example, our various experiences
before taking faith in the Daishonin's Buddhism are provisional
teachings outside the body of truth and correspond to functional-teaching and truth-gateway expedients.

The wondrous thing about the Mystic Law is that after embracing faith in the Gohonzon, not only do all our subsequent experiences shine as the secret and mystic expedient, but even our
experiences before taking faith come alive—as provisional teachings within the body of truth. President Toda often said: "All the
experiences of your life come alive. One comes to understand that
not a single instant was wasted. This is the great benefit of the
Mystic Law."

Suda: What a wonderful principle that is!

Ikeda: The doctrine of the secret and mystic expedient teaches us that even people who do not yet uphold the Mystic Law, though it is likely they don't know it themselves (for it is secret), are actually one with the Mystic Law (hence, 'mystic'). Because of this, in the depths of their being, they are seeking the Mystic Law.

In the "Orally Transmitted Teachings," Nichiren Daishonin says: "Even persons who are called great slanderers of the Law will in time come to accept and uphold Myoho-renge-kyo — this is the purpose of the 'Expedient Means' chapter of the Lotus Sutra" (GZ, 714).

There are many things I still would like to discuss about the secret and mystic expedient, but since it is a theme that runs throughout the Lotus Sutra, let us wait until another opportunity.

The point I want to make here is that, as noted earlier, the Buddhist concept of expedient means is also a superlative educational concept.

Suda: You once said: "True religious commitment and the true spirit of education are actually two manifestations of the same ideal of the complete liberation of the human being."[4]

Saito: This means that the true spirit of education and the spirit of the Lotus Sutra are two aspects of the same thing.

In his article "The Lotus Sutra and Value-Creating Education," President Makiguchi also writes: "In other words, it is my greatest joy and honor to declare that the philosophical core of value-creating education can be found in the Lotus Sutra's essence. My conviction is such that I can state unequivocally to not only Japan but the entire world that no true educational reform is possible unless it is based on the teaching of the Lotus Sutra."[5]

Ikeda: Mr. Makiguchi wanted to make the ideal of human education, which pioneering educators such as Switzerland's Johann Heinrich Pestalozzi and others had been advocating for years, take root in Japanese society. And Mr. Makiguchi, at the end of his quest for education that contributes to human happiness, reached the Lotus Sutra.

Pestalozzi wrote: "All pure powers of benediction brought forth by humanity are not gifts of skill or chance. They lie in the inner nature of all human beings, along with other inherent qualities. The development of these powers is the common necessity of all humankind."[6]

In pursuing this common necessity, Mr. Makiguchi advocated an educational revolution, and he further concluded that the only way to achieve it was through a religious revolution based on the Lotus Sutra.

Let us explore this educational spirit, this common wish of humanity. I recently read an interview with Professor Robert Thurman, chairman of the Department of Religion of Columbia University.

Saito: It's from a newsletter published by the SGI-USA Boston Research Center for the 21st Century. The article begins with a question: "How do you view the role of education in society, and what influenced your thinking on the subject?" Dr. Thurman replies: "I think the question should rather be: What is the role of society in education? Because in my view education is the purpose of human life."[7]

Ikeda: Dr. Thurman's reply continues, but I was deeply moved by his opening words. His profound view of humanity is apparent here. In other words, he views education not as a part or offshoot of society; it is an inherent part of human beings and their most fundamental endeavor. Human beings cannot exist apart from education, and that is why the relationship of teacher and student, mentor and disciple, is one of the most important things in life.

Suda: Dr. Thurman is using the term *education* in its broadest and deepest sense, not as a system or institution.

Ikeda: Yes. Dr. Thurman declares, "Education is the purpose of human life." To rephrase this, we might ask: For what purpose are human beings born? The answer is, to develop their lives to the fullest possible potential through education. In its ultimate form, this means to open the door to and show people the Buddha wisdom, to awaken them to it and guide them onto its path.

Saito: Professor Thurman continues: "Of course, what influenced me in [my view of education] is the teaching of the Buddha, which I perceive to be an educational teaching in the truest sense.... Buddhist practice really is to transform the individual and is thus part of the process of educating."[8]

Ikeda: A keen perception indeed. Human education and Buddhism are two aspects of the same reality. That is why Mr. Makiguchi's quest in the educational realm brought him to the Lotus Sutra and why I, based on the Lotus Sutra, actively promote a movement for education and culture.

Let us look at Buddhism as an educational movement in terms of the concept of expedient means. Clearly it is a movement emphasizing self-education with the aim of unlocking and developing our inherent Buddha nature while at the same time bringing forth diverse wisdom and using various expedient means to help others tap their Buddhahood. This development of potential, this education of oneself and others, is the noblest path a human being can ever pursue.

Endo: We could say, then, that the moment the enlightened Shakyamuni broke through his hesitation, resolved to preach the True Law to people mired in suffering, and first employed expedient means encompasses the essence of what life as a human is fundamentally supposed to be.

Ikeda: Shakyamuni's life after his enlightenment was a continuation of that moment. Expedient means represent the compassion, wisdom and action to lead others to happiness. They can never be fixed into any one pattern; they embody the spirit of challenging oneself to the very limits to find ways to lead people to happiness on a wider and more profound level.

THE SPIRIT OF RAISING CAPABLE PEOPLE

Suda: In our SGI activities, it is important that we all strive to educate ourselves and also help train and raise others.

Ikeda: That is a very crucial point. Propagating the teachings as well as fostering and raising capable people are all activities that accord with the Lotus Sutra's spirit. Other SGI cultural and social activities only take on profound significance when they contribute to developing people of ability and bring more and more people into contact with Buddhism.

In "Expedient Means," Shakyamuni states:

> at the start I took a vow,
> hoping to make all persons
> equal to me, without any distinction between us. (LS2, 36)

The Buddha vows to elevate all people to the same state of life as his own. This is the spirit to raise capable people, to enable people to develop to their fullest potential. This is also the spirit underlying the mentor–disciple relationship.

Of course, since we also strive to keep growing and developing ourselves, the determination to bring others not only to our level but above and beyond is the true spirit of the Buddha's vow to "make all persons equal to me, without any distinction between us."

Saito: By contrast, not only do the priests of Nichiren Shoshu under Nikken care nothing for educating others, they refuse to recognize those who surpass them in any way. This is completely opposed to the Lotus Sutra's spirit. Religions gone astray behave in this manner.

Ikeda: The true essence of humanism lies in our compassion and earnest commitment to pray and exert ourselves for the growth of our fellow members, particularly those newer in faith. The SGI is a humanistic organization. It isn't run on authority or orders from above. It moves forward with the joy of being in contact with genuine humanity.

The poetic genius of the great Russian writer Aleksandr Pushkin was nurtured by the humanity of his old nurse, a humble serf. He called her Mother and trusted her from the bottom of his heart. The folk stories he heard from her, told in the words of the common people, inspired his writings that have moved so many to this day.

Similarly, with the support and encouragement of her beloved teacher, Anne Sullivan Macy, Helen Keller, who could neither see nor hear, gained entry into Harvard's Radcliffe College. Ms. Macy devoted her life to serving as Helen's eyes and ears, sacrificing the freedom to pursue her own talents and potential.

In her later years, Anne Macy, along with Helen, was offered an honorary doctorate. But she refused, saying she was overjoyed that her student Helen received the honor, and that was enough for her. She did eventually accept an honorary doctorate the following year—a distinction that came just four years before her death. When Ms. Macy died, Helen Keller vowed to carry on the life of service her teacher had devoted to her. In her teacher's spirit, she launched a global movement to assist the blind and deaf and improve their lot.

Anne Sullivan Macy was a dedicated teacher, a woman who spent her entire life helping behind the scenes. Isn't this the true portrait of a champion of human education? In that sense, how noble and praiseworthy are our SGI members, who cherish the Mystic Law in their hearts and strive wholeheartedly day and night to educate and foster capable people.

In "Expedient Means," we find the passage, "This Law cannot be described, words fall silent before it" (LS2, 25). Just as the greatness of the Mystic Law cannot be described in words, the greatness of a life dedicated to the Mystic Law is also beyond description.

Saito: Speaking of educating and fostering others, I will never forget the words of Lu Xun that you've quoted: "In life, it is a joy to nurture others, even though one knows that in doing so, shedding one drop of blood at a time, one grows weaker and frailer."[9]

Ikeda: I am nurturing and educating our youth today in exactly the same spirit, and I hope you will do so as well. This is the way for a person who believes in the Lotus Sutra to live — the path of the oneness of mentor and disciple. When mentor and disciple work as one to promote an educational movement that inspires and awakens people's humanity and nourishes all humankind, their unstinting contribution to society exemplifies the principles that Buddhahood retains the nine worlds and the nine worlds have the potential for Buddhahood. It becomes a dynamic demonstration of the secret and mystic expedient.

NOTES

1. Tsunesaburo Makiguchi, *Soka Kyoikugaku Taikei* (The System of Value-Creating Pedagogy) (Tokyo: Seikyo Shimunsha, 1980), vol. 4, p. 68.

2. *Toda Josei Zenshu* (Tokyo: Seikyo Shimunsha, 1982), vol. 2, p. 69.

3. Ibid. (Tokyo: Seikyo Shimunsha, 1985), vol. 5, p. 279.

4. At a gathering of Soka School alumni, November 1990.

5. *"Soka Kyoikugaku Taikei Kogai"* (An Outline of the System of Value-Creating Pedagogy), p. 410.

6. Translated from German: Johann Heinrich Pestalozzi, *Die Abendstunde eines Einsiedlers* (1780), cited in the appendix of *Sekai Kyoikugaku Senshu* (A Collection of World Pedagogy), trans. Satoru Umene (Tokyo: Meiji Tosho Shuppan, 1971), vol. 35, p. 269.

7. "Boston Research Center for the 21st Century Newsletter," Spring 1995, No. 3, p. 7.

8. Ibid.

9. Translated from Japanese: *Lu Xun, Rojin no Shogai* (The Life of Lu Xun), trans. Jiro Kaneko and Shin'ichi Ohara (Tokyo: Toho Shoten, 1978), p. 283.

7   The Revelation of the Single Buddha Vehicle: Opening the Door to the Oneness of Mentor and Disciple

Ikeda: President Toda's deepest wish, his constant concern, was to elevate the inner state of life of all humanity. He once declared: "We, the members of the Soka Gakkai, are the Bodhisattvas of the Earth; we are envoys of the Thus Come One, of Nichiren Daishonin. With that conviction, we must carry out the work of the Thus Come One. What does that mean? It means to bring all people to the state of Buddhahood—in other words, to elevate the character of all humanity to the very highest level."

Mr. Toda's goal was to lead all humanity to Buddhahood. On another occasion, he said that the single Buddha vehicle revealed in the principle of 'the replacement of the three vehicles with the one vehicle' represents the supreme state of life to which all humanity should aspire. Let us now examine the replacement of the three vehicles with the one vehicle, using Mr. Toda's insights as our guide.

THE UNIFICATION OF THE TEACHINGS AND PRACTITIONERS OF THE THREE VEHICLES

> "Shariputra, the Thus Come Ones have only a single Buddha vehicle which they employ in order to preach the Law to living beings. They do not have any other vehicle, a second one or a third one...." (LS2, 31)

Saito: Yes, let's begin. The concept of the replacement of the three vehicles with the one vehicle summarizes the core substance of Shakyamuni's preaching—which begins to be revealed in "Expedient Means"—in the theoretical teaching (first half) of the Lotus Sutra. Here, Shakyamuni explains the real function of the three vehicles and reveals that there is only one true vehicle.

The 'three vehicles' refers to the vehicles of Learning, Realization and Bodhisattva—in other words, the respective teachings for becoming a voice-hearer, *pratyekabuddha* and bodhisattva. The teachings of the Buddha are likened to vehicles because they convey people to a higher state of being.

The 'one vehicle' means 'the one and only teaching.' Since the Buddha expounds his teaching solely so that all people may attain Buddhahood, it is also called the Buddha vehicle or the one Buddha vehicle. It can also be interpreted to mean the conveyance by which the Buddha himself attained enlightenment. The one vehicle teaches the path the Buddha himself followed and furnishes us with that very same means to follow that path.

Endo: In "Expedient Means," the one vehicle is expounded in terms of the four aspects of the Buddha wisdom: opening, showing, awakening and causing to enter. In short, the Buddha has only one teaching and it is to open, show, awaken and cause all living beings to enter the path of the Buddha wisdom. These four aspects together represent the 'one great reason'—the sole reason—why Buddhas appear in the world.

The Buddha wisdom refers to the Buddha's enlightenment. In "Expedient Means," it is called "the wisdom embracing all species" (LS2, 32), since it is the supreme wisdom that comprehends the ultimate truth of all things. The enlightenment achieved through gaining entry to this wisdom is called "supreme perfect enlightenment," or *anuttara-samyak-sambodhi*. The one vehicle teaches this Buddha wisdom.

Suda: Because it transcends words and thoughts, however, the true meaning of this Buddha wisdom is difficult to grasp. Moreover, human beings are hindered by various attachments and delusions. Were the Buddha to simply preach the one vehicle according to his own mind—that is, according to his understanding as a Buddha—without any introduction or preparation, his audience would most likely fail to comprehend his true intent [that of opening, showing, revealing and causing all beings to enter the path of the Buddha wisdom]. Many may refuse to accept the teaching or may be filled with doubt and fall into evil paths as a result. Hence the necessity for the Buddha to preach his teaching in a way that matched the capacity of his audience—that is, in accord with others' minds.

The three vehicles is the teaching the Buddha expounded in response to the different life-states of his audience via the power of expedient means. The principle of the three vehicles does not teach the Buddha wisdom. Nor is it the Buddha's true intent or purpose. It is, however, an indispensable means for preparing people for the ultimate teaching of the one supreme vehicle, which is the Buddha's true purpose.

Ikeda: "Expedient Means" makes it absolutely clear that the true intent of the Buddha in teaching the three vehicles was to teach the one vehicle. This clarification is called 'the replacement of the three vehicles with the one vehicle.' It stresses that the Buddha teaches only one vehicle, and that there are not two vehicles or three vehicles.

Shakyamuni gives explicit expression to the fact that there is only one vehicle, in the passage: "The Thus Come Ones have only a single Buddha vehicle which they employ in order to preach the Law to living beings. They do not have any other vehicle, a second one or a third one" (LS2, 31).

The three vehicles are meanwhile put into their proper perspective in the passage: "The Buddhas, utilizing the power of expedient means, apply distinctions to the one Buddha vehicle and preach it as though it were three" (LS2, 32).

In other words, the three vehicles is a way in which the Buddha divided up the teachings of the single Buddha vehicle as an expedient means to lead people to the truth.

"Expedient Means" repeatedly and strongly emphasizes that the Buddha's true intent lies solely in teaching the one Buddha vehicle. The revelation that the three vehicles are merely expedient means and that only the one Buddha vehicle is true is also called 'the unification of the three vehicles within the one vehicle.' There are two aspects of this unification—'the unification of the practitioners' and 'the unification of the teachings.'

Saito: The unification of the teachings, as you have just explained, is the unification of the three vehicles within the one vehicle. After they are thus unified, the teachings of the three vehicles are put in their proper place within the one vehicle, and each has its own significance. Each is still valid as a partial truth or view.

The unification of the practitioners, meanwhile, is the revelation that all who are taught and converted by the teaching of the one vehicle are bodhisattvas without exception. "Expedient Means" states, "The Buddhas, the Thus Come Ones, simply teach and convert the bodhisattvas..." (LS2, 31); and "I employ only the single vehicle way / to teach and convert the bodhisattvas, / I have no voice-hearer disciples" (LS2, 45). In such passages, the Buddha reveals the single Buddha vehicle and calls out to all living beings —specifically the followers of the two vehicles [the voice-hearers and *pratyekabuddhas*]—to embrace this single vehicle. By doing so, these practitioners of the two vehicles are united with the bodhisattvas; that is, they become bodhisattvas, too.

A bodhisattva is a person who aspires for enlightenment or, from a deeper perspective, a person whose attainment of Buddhahood is assured. Such a person is also referred to as a *mahasattva*, or "great being."

Ikeda: In short, by declaring unequivocally that the Buddha teaches only the one Buddha vehicle, the sutra is also saying that all people are bodhisattvas. The practitioners of the two vehicles are thus also bodhisattvas and as such can attain enlightenment. The unification of the practitioners emphasizes that the teachings of the one vehicle enable all people to achieve Buddhahood. Key to this is the doctrine of 'the enlightenment of the two vehicles' expounded in the Lotus Sutra.

I think the concept of 'the replacement of the three vehicles with the one vehicle' is easier to grasp when considered from these two aspects of the 'unification of the teachings' and the 'unification of the practitioners.' Why don't we concentrate our discussions in this chapter on the 'unification of the practitioners,' in other words, 'the enlightenment of the two vehicles'?

Saito: I think that's a good idea. After all, the concept that persons of the two vehicles can attain Buddhahood is found only in the Lotus Sutra.

THE ENLIGHTENMENT OF THE TWO VEHICLES AND THE MUTUAL POSSESSION OF THE TEN WORLDS

> *Shariputra, you should know*
> *that at the start I took a vow,*
> *hoping to make all persons*
> *equal to me, without any distinction between us,*
> *and what I long ago hoped for*
> *has now been fulfilled.*
> *I have converted all living beings*
> *and caused them all to enter the Buddha way.* (LS2, 36)

Endo: I learned about the enlightenment of the two vehicles each time I studied for a Soka Gakkai study examination. My seniors were always warning me not to develop tendencies like people of the two vehicles! We generally have a fairly negative image of such people as highly intelligent but conceited about their knowledge or self-centered and caring only for their own salvation, lacking the compassion to save others.

Ikeda: That doesn't really do them justice, I think. Certainly those aspects of the two vehicles cannot be denied, but for the most part, people with those characteristics are not really of the two vehicles at all, regardless of their pretensions. In reality, they lack the fierce seeking spirit and thirst for truth that are hallmarks of persons of the two vehicles.

President Toda offered a somewhat broader interpretation to facilitate understanding, saying that in contemporary times people of the two vehicles correspond to outstanding intellectuals, people who should by rights be treasures of their society. We might imagine them to be great scholars or philosophers who have received several Nobel prizes. Moreover, they are people who have abandoned all concern for fame and fortune and who strive to eliminate selfishness and greed. They are individuals of superior character. In this respect, it is no easy thing to become a person of the two vehicles!

Suda: Why were such superior disciples of the Buddha as the voice-hearers and *pratyekabuddhas* [people of Learning and Realization] deemed to be eternally incapable of attaining Buddhahood? This is very strange indeed, when we come to think of it.

Endo: Yes, and until the Lotus Sutra was preached, people of the two vehicles were bitterly scorned. They were said to be like scorched seeds from which the sprout of the Buddha nature would never appear. It was considered preferable to fall into hell than to be counted among those of the two vehicles.

Saito: The ideal for which people of the two vehicles strove and practiced was that of 'annihilating the consciousness and reducing the body to ashes,' the extinction of body and mind. They aimed for a state in which their physical body, the source of all earthly desires, and their mind, which allowed them to feel pain and suffering, were utterly extinguished. Nichiren Daishonin states, "They [the people of the two vehicles] seek to rid themselves of both body and mind and become like empty space" (GZ, 393). The paradox is that if they achieve their goal, no self would remain to attain Buddhahood.

Suda: Comparisons are often made between those of the two vehicles and the bodhisattvas, who together as a group form the three vehicles. Bodhisattvas seek to benefit others, while people of the two vehicles seek only to benefit themselves. This was why it was regarded as impossible for people of the two vehicles to attain Buddhahood.

Ikeda: People of the two vehicles are said to despise the world of the six paths [the first six of the Ten Worlds from Hell to Heaven], and so once they have achieved release from them and reached a state "like empty space," they do not return to the mundane world of suffering and strife. They do not return to try and save those remaining in the six paths. Indeed, they completely forget that they owe a debt to all living beings.

Nichiren Daishonin wrote: "They have no desire to save other beings, for they wish never to return to the six paths" (GZ, 434); and "They fall into the pit of emancipation and can benefit neither themselves nor others" (WND, 228). To abandon those whom you are meant to save is not Buddhism. If you do that, you cannot save yourself, either. That is why the Daishonin says, "To arouse the mind of the two vehicles for even an instant is even worse than committing any of the ten evil acts or five cardinal sins" (GZ, 435).

Suda: It's only natural, I guess, that people might take the attitude "Let's forget about these ungrateful people of the two vehicles and concentrate instead on becoming bodhisattvas!"

Ikeda: Here, of course, you're referring to the bodhisattvas of the three vehicles. There is a serious contradiction, however, in the belief that those of the two vehicles cannot attain Buddhahood while bodhisattvas can. If we probe this issue more deeply, we will come to understand why it was necessary to preach the Lotus Sutra.

Suppose we were to forget about the people of two vehicles and go ahead and become bodhisattvas. By doing so, however, we would be just as lacking in compassion as those of the two vehicles when they turned their backs on people of the six paths.

The bodhisattva makes four universal vows in the pursuit of Buddhahood. One is the vow to save innumerable living beings. If bodhisattvas desert those of the two vehicles, leaving them in a state where they are eternally incapable of attaining Buddhahood, then they abandon this vow to save others and block off the path for their own enlightenment as well. The Daishonin writes: "If the persons of the two vehicles cannot attain Buddhahood, then neither can the bodhisattvas, because the bodhisattvas have made a vow to save innumerable beings" (GZ, 589).

In the pre-Lotus Sutra teachings, we find assertions that bodhisattvas can attain enlightenment but people of the two vehicles cannot; bodhisattvas rejoice at this and those of the two vehicles grieve, while all of this is beyond the conception of those of the worlds of Humanity and Heaven (cf. GZ, 401).

But the bodhisattvas are deluding themselves here; they actually have no reason to rejoice in the idea that they alone will attain Buddhahood.

Endo: Yes, you're right.

Ikeda: Why did people fall victim to this misguided, contradictory view? Ultimately, it's because no sutra other than the Lotus Sutra expounds the mutual possession of the Ten Worlds. This doctrine is found only in the Lotus Sutra.

Suda: The Ten Worlds are the ten states of being ranging from the world of Hell to the world of Buddhahood. The mutual possession of the Ten Worlds means that each is endowed with the other nine worlds. As the Daishonin says, "The mutual possession of the Ten Worlds means that each of the Ten Worlds contains within it the other nine" (GZ, 400).

Saito: The main point of the mutual possession of the Ten Worlds is that the nine worlds are endowed with Buddhahood and that Buddhahood is endowed with the nine worlds. The theoretical teaching of the Lotus Sutra emphasizes the first aspect — the nine worlds are endowed with Buddhahood. It reveals that the nine worlds, including the two vehicles, contain the world of Buddhahood.

Ikeda: Exactly. Where is the world of Buddhahood found? It is found within the worlds of the two vehicles. And where are the worlds of the two vehicles found? Just as certainly they, too, are found within the worlds of Bodhisattva and Buddhahood.

Saito: Based on the perspective of life embodied in the doctrine of the mutual possession of the Ten Worlds, the bodhisattva is in no position to criticize or revile the people of the two vehicles, because those two worlds or states of being exist within the life of the bodhisattva as well.

Endo: If people of the two vehicles cannot attain Buddhahood, it means the life-states of the two vehicles existing within the bodhisattva do not attain Buddhahood. Since these elements are an indivisible part of life and cannot be cut out and discarded, it means that bodhisattvas themselves cannot attain enlightenment.

Suda: That is what the Daishonin means when he says: "Bodhisattvas are endowed with the worlds of the two vehicles, so if the persons of the two vehicles cannot attain Buddhahood, then neither can the bodhisattvas" (GZ, 421).

Ikeda: Yes. And this principle applies to each of the Ten Worlds. As the Daishonin says:

> If the worlds of the two vehicles do not attain Buddhahood, then the worlds of the two vehicles within each of the other eight worlds will not attain Buddhahood. And if the worlds of the two vehicles within each of the other eight worlds do not attain Buddhahood, then none of the other eight worlds will attain Buddhahood. (GZ, 522)

If people of the two vehicles cannot attain Buddhahood, then it would be impossible even for a Buddha to be a Buddha, given that the worlds of the two vehicles within the world of Buddhahood could not attain Buddhahood.

In the pre-Lotus Sutra teachings, the causes and effects of each of the Ten Worlds are taught separately. The attainment of Buddhahood expounded in those earlier sutras is not of real substance but only a "shadow" of the real thing. The Lotus Sutra teaches that each of the Ten Worlds mutually possesses the causes and effects of all other worlds. Therefore, the attainment of Buddhahood for all living beings in all of the Ten Worlds is made possible for the first time by the Lotus Sutra. This is the criterion by which we can determine whether a sutra preaches the ultimate truth: Does it teach the mutual possession of the Ten Worlds?

Endo: Yes, it's precisely as the Daishonin declares: "The Lotus Sutra teaches none other than this. While the causes and effects of the Ten Worlds were revealed in the pre-Lotus Sutra teachings, only the Lotus Sutra establishes the mutual possession of the causes and effects of all Ten Worlds" (GZ, 401).

Saito: So, as mentioned earlier, the bodhisattvas really couldn't afford to be indifferent to the grief of those of the two vehicles when the latter were told they could never attain enlightenment.

Ikeda: Yes, and that's a crucial point. Nichiren Daishonin writes: "The persons of the two vehicles are not the only ones who should grieve when it is announced that they will never attain Buddhahood; know that we, too, must grieve with them" (GZ, 522).

And he expresses his own sentiments: "The failure of others to attain Buddhahood is my failure to attain Buddhahood, and the attainment of Buddhahood by others is my attainment of Buddhahood. The birth in the Pure Land by other ordinary people is my birth in the Pure Land" (GZ, 401).

Before the doctrine of the mutual possession of the Ten Worlds was expounded, the problems and concerns of others were regarded as something divorced and separate from oneself. But with the teaching of the mutual possession of the Ten Worlds, people came to realize that the attainment of Buddhahood by others was their own attainment of Buddhahood, while if others could not attain Buddhahood, then neither could they themselves. This dramatically transformed people's view of life and the world.

The misfortune of others is our misfortune. Our happiness is the happiness of others. To see ourselves in others and feel an inner oneness and sense of unity with them represents a fundamental revolution in the way we view and live our lives. Therefore, discriminating against another person is the same as discriminating against oneself. When we hurt another, we are hurting ourselves. And when we respect others, we respect and elevate our own lives as well.

Saito: In other words, by embracing the philosophy of life embodied in the mutual possession of the Ten Worlds, we can transcend discrimination and achieve true equality.

Ikeda: That's correct. As Nichiren Daishonin says, "The provisional sutras teach inequality, but the Lotus Sutra teaches equality" (GZ, 816). The Lotus Sutra doesn't preach equality as just a slogan; it teaches a way to happiness for oneself and others alike, addressing the conditions of our lives on a fundamental level and how those life-conditions are expressed through the way we live our lives.

The Daishonin also tells us that the Latter Day of the Law is "the time for the widespread propagation of the Great Vehicle, the Law in which all things are equal, Nam-myoho-renge-kyo" (GZ, 816).

Endo: Bodhisattva Never Disparaging, one of the characters of the Lotus Sutra, through his behavior and actions expresses the life view implicit in the doctrine of the mutual possession of the Ten Worlds. Though he is scorned and persecuted, he continues to show reverence to the arrogant members of the four kinds of believers [monks, nuns, laymen and laywomen].

Ikeda: Yes, we will be discussing Bodhisattva Never Disparaging in greater detail later on. In the "Orally Transmitted Teachings," the Daishonin describes the actions of Bodhisattva Never Disparaging as "reverence simultaneously for oneself and others" (GZ, 769). When Bodhisattva Never Disparaging pays reverence to others, the Buddha nature in others pays reverence to him. This is a very profound teaching.

The English poet John Donne writes:

> No man is an island, entire of itself; every man is a piece
> of the continent, a part of the main; if a clod be washed
> away by the sea, Europe is the less, as well as if a pro-
> montory were, as well as if a manor of thy friends or of
> thine own were; any man's death diminishes me, because
> I am involved in mankind; and therefore never send to
> know for whom the bell tolls; it tolls for thee.[1]

Both you and I are part of the continent of humanity, says Donne. Let's develop a life state as vast as a great continent, regarding the fortune or misfortune of others as our own. In fact, Mr. Toda asserted that striving to develop an even greater life state, one as vast as the universe, is the aim of the single Buddha vehicle and the heart of the replacement of the three vehicles with the one vehicle. Mr. Toda's wish was to elevate the spiritual state of all humanity to that level.

Suda: I'm awed by Mr. Toda's determination. The enlightenment of the two vehicles has surprising relevance and significance for contemporary society, doesn't it? I hadn't fully appreciated this before.

Ikeda: But we must remember that what we are discussing here is the mutual possession of the Ten Worlds expounded in the theoretical teaching of the Lotus Sutra. Here, as I mentioned earlier, the emphasis is only on the nine worlds being endowed with Buddhahood, rather than the aspect of Buddhahood being endowed with the nine worlds. The true mutual possession of the Ten Worlds is expressed in its full and perfect form only in the "Life Span" chapter in the essential teaching of the Lotus Sutra, when the eternal nature of the Buddha's life is revealed. But let's discuss this on another occasion.

Suda: Shakyamuni described the one Buddha vehicle as "the Great Vehicle, the Law in which all things are equal" (LS2, 35). How overjoyed those of the two vehicles must have been when they learned of this supreme teaching, this supreme way of life!

Endo: The sutra describes Shariputra as being filled with irrepressible joy and leaping to his feet to make a gesture of reverence to Shakyamuni: "At that time Shariputra's mind danced with joy. Then he immediately stood up, [and] pressed his palms together" (LS3, 47).

Saito: It must have been no ordinary joy for this great scholar, esteemed as "foremost in wisdom," to leap to his feet. This scene represents the revitalization of the voice-hearers through the Lotus Sutra.

Ikeda: His mind was transformed at its very foundation. Shariputra then pronounces his acceptance of the single Buddha vehicle:

> Now I have heard from the Buddha what I had never heard before, a Law never known in the past, and it has ended all my doubts and regrets. My body and mind are at ease and I have gained a wonderful feeling of peace and security. Today at last I understand that truly I am the Buddha's son, born of the Buddha's mouth, born through conversion to the Law, gaining my share of the Buddha's Law! (LS3, 48)

In Mahayana Buddhism, "Buddha's son"—which may also be rendered variously as "Buddha's child" or "child of the Buddha" —refers to the bodhisattva. Once Shariputra believed and understood the single Buddha vehicle, he was transformed from a voice-hearer into a bodhisattva.

Endo: The same thing happens later in the sutra when the four great voice-hearer disciples—Mahakashyapa, Maudgalyayana and the others—hear the parable of the three carts and the burning house and finally grasp the meaning of the replacement of the three vehicles with the one Buddha vehicle.

In this parable, related in the "Parables and Similes" chapter, the house of a wealthy man catches fire. His children are playing inside the burning house oblivious to the danger they are in. He resorts to an expedient device to lure them outside. He promises them three carts—one pulled by a sheep, one by a deer and one by an ox. But when his children rush outside, he actually gives them a much finer cart adorned with jewels—a single great white ox cart.

In the parable, the burning house represents the threefold world, and the flames, the sufferings of birth and death. The rich man is the Buddha, who appears in the world to save people; the children represent all living beings; and the games in which they are absorbed are worldly pleasures. The three carts originally promised represent the three provisional vehicles of Learning, Realization and Bodhisattva, and the great white ox cart symbolizes the supreme vehicle of Buddhahood, that is, the Lotus Sutra.

In the "Belief and Understanding" chapter, the voice-hearers declare:

> Now we have become
> voice-hearers in truth,
> for we will take the voice of the Buddha way
> and cause it to be heard by all. (LS4, 94)

In other words, they are transformed from voice-hearers who merely hear the teachings into genuine voice-hearers who seek to convey the teachings to others.

Ikeda: Yes. Once the three vehicles are unified into the one Buddha vehicle, the voice-hearers can carry out their original mission as envoys of the Buddha, just as they are.

Saito: The voice-hearers changed in other ways as well. Whereas before they had been accused of ingratitude, they now praise the great mercy of the Buddha, saying:

> The World-Honored One in his great mercy
> makes use of a rare thing,
> in pity and compassion teaching and converting,
> bringing benefit to us.
> In numberless millions of kalpas
> who could ever repay him? (LS4, 95)

This represents a 180-degree change in the voice-hearers' orientation.

Suda: Shakyamuni explains to the followers of the two vehicles:

> What you are practicing
> is the bodhisattva way,
> and as you gradually advance in practice and learning
> you are all certain to attain Buddhahood. (LS5, 106)

He also informs them:

> Therefore the bodhisattvas
> pose as voice-hearers or pratyekabuddhas,...
> to convert the different kinds of living beings....
> Inwardly, in secret, the sons [of the Buddha] act
> as bodhisattvas,
> but outwardly they show themselves as voice-hearers.
> They seem to be lessening desires out of hatred
> for birth and death,
> but in truth they are purifying the Buddha lands. (LS8, 146)

Ikeda: Shakyamuni is telling them: "You may think you are voice-hearers, but in fact you are bodhisattvas. Playing the role of voice-hearers, you lead people to the Buddha way."

THE SINGLE BUDDHA VEHICLE REPRESENTS THE PATH OF THE ONENESS OF MENTOR AND DISCIPLE

Suda: "Expedient Means" also emphasizes that the single Buddha vehicle is a teaching solely for bodhisattvas. A frequent source of confusion here is the distinction between the bodhisattvas who have accepted the single Buddha vehicle and the bodhisattvas still of the three vehicles. Are they the same or not? And if they are different, how are they different?

Endo: This issue led to divided schools of opinion in Chinese

Buddhism over whether there were three vehicles or four vehicles. The parable of the three carts and the burning house detailed in "Parables and Similes" supports the doctrine of 'the replacement of the three vehicles with the one vehicle,' as we have already touched on. Without going into too much detail, the vehicle of the voice-hearers is represented by a sheep cart, the vehicle of the *pratyekabuddhas* by a deer cart and the vehicle of the bodhisattva by an ox cart. The single Buddha vehicle, meanwhile, is likened to a great white ox cart.

If the vehicle of the bodhisattva (the ox cart) and the one Buddha vehicle (the great white ox cart) are the same, then there are only three carts in all; but if they (the two ox carts) are different, then there are four vehicles. This is the nub of the controversy. The Great Teacher T'ien-t'ai of China took the view that there were four carts.

Ikeda: This is no doubt a many-faceted issue, but in at least one respect, may I suggest the following interpretation? The disciples of the Buddha who practiced the three vehicles prior to the revelation of the single Buddha vehicle were following the way of mentor and disciple after a fashion. But the doctrine of the replacement of the three vehicles with the one vehicle teaches us to follow the way of the oneness of mentor and disciple.

Saito: What is the significance of this evolution from 'the way of mentor and disciple' to 'the way of the oneness of mentor and disciple'?

Ikeda: Before the revelation of the one Buddha vehicle, the bodhisattvas who were followers of the Bodhisattva vehicle maintained a separate identity from that of the followers of the other two vehicles of Learning and Realization, whom they believed could never attain enlightenment. Because they viewed each of the Ten Worlds as separate from one another, the bodhisattvas were not only unable to save other living beings, but they also could not attain Buddhahood themselves.

But the Buddha's wish is to enable all living beings to attain enlightenment. Though there is always inevitably some degree of disparity in the state of life of the mentor and that of the disciple, in the case of the bodhisattvas of the three vehicles, the very spirit, aspiration and philosophy of mentor and disciple are fundamentally irreconcilable. On the other hand, the bodhisattvas who embrace the one Buddha vehicle after the three vehicles have been put in their proper perspective base themselves on the principle of the mutual possession of the Ten Worlds — that all living beings can equally attain enlightenment, including the now-transformed voice-hearers. Armed with this profound philosophy, they then embark on the great challenge to lead all living beings to enlightenment. Here, for the first time, they enter the same path as the Buddha. In this fundamental commitment, mentor and disciple become comrades who share the same goal and are bound in a relationship as a senior and junior in faith traveling a shared path. Advancing in such unity — with such oneness of heart and mind — is the true way of mentor and disciple.

Saito: I see. That explains it very clearly.

Ikeda: In this struggle to dive into the "ocean" of society and strive to bring everyone aboard the "great ship" bound for happiness, the Buddha, too, is a bodhisattva. Explaining the mutual possession of the Ten Worlds, the Daishonin says: "The Buddha also dwells in the stage of practice, re-entering the world of Bodhisattva. Though he has actually attained the highest state of perfect enlightenment, he adopts the state of near-perfect enlightenment" (GZ, 401).

In any event, the mentor's intent, as expressed in "Expedient Means," is "to make all persons equal to me, without any distinction between us" (LS2, 36). The Buddha's compassion is such that his goal is to bring all living beings to a state of life identical to his own. Another passage in this chapter tells us:

The original vow of the Buddhas
was that the Buddha way, which they themselves practice,
should be shared universally among living beings
so that they too may attain this same way. (LS2, 41)

The "original vow" of the Buddhas is to enable all people to
walk their same path toward enlightenment.

Of course, the practitioners of the three vehicles of the sutras
before the Lotus Sutra also believed in and followed the Buddha.
And in their fashion, they followed the way of mentor and disciple.
But these disciples always felt an unbridgeable gap between them
and their mentor: the disciple was the disciple and the Buddha
was the Buddha. The disciple did not know the mind of the mentor. The Lotus Sutra, however, broke through this deluded belief.

The replacement of the three vehicles with the one vehicle
engendered a fundamental transformation in the mind and the
way of life of the disciple—a transformation from the way of
mentor and disciple to the way of the oneness of mentor and disciple.

Suda: That's made things very clear. As mentioned earlier, when
Shariputra heard the teaching of the single Buddha vehicle, he realized that he was a true child of the Buddha. "Child of the Buddha"
also seems to me symbolic of the oneness of mentor and disciple.

Ikeda: Yes. President Toda often said: "A blacksmith's apprentice is a
blacksmith; a fishmonger's trainee is a fishmonger. In the same way,
the Buddha's disciple is a Buddha. It all works out very neatly....
We are actively sharing the teachings with others just as the Daishonin instructed, so we are the disciples of the Daishonin."

Mr. Toda also repeatedly emphasized that we are children of the
Buddha. Whether aware of it or not, a lion's cub is a lion and a
child of the Buddha is a Buddha. This is an incontrovertible fact;
a self-evident reality. When we are profoundly aware of this reality,
we have entered the path of the oneness of mentor and disciple.

Endo: "Child of the Buddha" transcends all distinctions such as voice-hearer, *pratyekabuddha* or bodhisattva, though in terms of action, I would agree that it refers specifically to the bodhisattva. It seems to me that the mentor's compassion to elevate his disciples to the same state of life as his own, and the disciples' determination to move forward one in mind with their mentor, are both encompassed by the expression, "child of the Buddha."

Ikeda: I think that is exactly right. To the Buddha, all beings of the Ten Worlds are his children. But among all those children, those who embrace and uphold the Mystic Law can be called his "true children."

"The Emergence of the Treasure Tower" chapter of the Lotus Sutra states:

> And if in future existences
> one can read and uphold this sutra,
> he will be a true son of the Buddha. (LSII, 181)

Saito: When we consider that the Lotus Sutra is a scripture expounded for those living in the age after the Buddha's passing, I think we can identify the true children of the Buddha as the Bodhisattvas of the Earth.

Ikeda: Yes. In the "Orally Transmitted Teachings," Nichiren Daishonin says: "The 'children' are the Bodhisattvas of the Earth and the 'father' is Shakyamuni" (GZ, 803). Those disciples who cherish the same vow, the same sense of responsibility, as their mentor — in other words, those disciples who stand up united as one with their mentor — are the Bodhisattvas of the Earth.

The Daishonin writes, "If you are of the same mind as Nichiren, you must be a Bodhisattva of the Earth" (WND, 385). There is special significance to the Daishonin's phrase "of the same mind."

The SGI, whose members have made the Daishonin's vow their own, working tirelessly to promote kosen-rufu, is an organization of the Bodhisattvas of the Earth carrying out the mission they pledged themselves to in the infinite past. It is a gathering of disciples indivisibly united with the Daishonin.

Endo: But the priesthood refused to let us say the SGI members are Bodhisattvas of the Earth. Instead, they insist thay lay people are merely the "followers" of the Bodhisattvas of the Earth.

Suda: If we are to be called followers, then we are the Daishonin's proud true followers. We are certainly not the followers of a corrupt priesthood.

Saito: I wonder how the priesthood interprets the Daishonin's declaration, "Were they not Bodhisattvas of the Earth, they could not chant the daimoku" (WND, 385).

Suda: The twenty-sixth high priest, Nichikan, also emphasized that striving to attain the same state of life as Nichiren Daishonin is the very essence of the Daishonin's Buddhism. He writes, "Through the power of the Mystic Law, we ourselves manifest the life of the founder, Nichiren Daishonin."[2] He also said, "When we chant Nam-myoho-renge-kyo with faith in the Gohonzon, our lives immediately become the Gohonzon of 'three thousand realms in a single moment of life,' the entity of the founder, Nichiren Daishonin."[3]

Endo: The priests of the Nikken sect, in direct violation of that spirit, are determined to prevent people from becoming one with the Daishonin. They must think it very much to their disadvantage to have followers advancing as one with the Daishonin, along the same path.

Suda: Yes, it seems they will do anything to disrupt the perfectly natural unity of mentor and disciple, wishing to insinuate themselves into the resulting fissure, so that they can dominate and control people. This is in direct contradiction to the Daishonin's teaching that ordinary people are endowed with the supremely noble state of Buddhahood, just as they are. It also runs counter to the teachings of Nichikan, who faithfully carried on the Daishonin's teaching.

Saito: Even the term *original Buddha* has become a tool in the hands of the priests of the Nikken sect to establish their authority. Their scheme is to elevate the authority of the high priest and of the priesthood overall by attempting to make people regard the Daishonin as some sort of transcendent being utterly separated from mortal human beings.

Ikeda: They act as if they revere the Daishonin, but in fact they are betraying his most profound intent. They are transforming a teaching of supreme respect for human beings into a teaching of the most deplorable contempt for human beings. They want to destroy the path of the oneness of mentor and disciple as taught by the Daishonin because of their own arrogant disdain for the laity.

Dostoevsky comments astutely on this same impulse: "Many very proud people like to believe in God, especially those who despise other people.... The reason is obvious. They turn to God to avoid doing homage to men...; to do homage to God is not so humiliating."[4]

Here Dostoevsky reveals his keen understanding of the workings of the human psyche.

Saito: We only have to change the word *God* in this passage to the Nikken-sect expression "the transcendent original Buddha"—which they use to portray the Daishonin as residing on a plane utterly divorced from the realm of common mortals—and we would have a perfect description of the Nikken sect.

Endo: What they pay homage to is not really the teachings of the Daishonin but their own ambition and pride.

Ikeda: Nothing is more foolish than to be taken in by such corrupt people. It is important that we see through them.

The oneness of mentor and disciple is the very heart of the Lotus Sutra and the essence of Nichiren Daishonin's teachings, yet the priests try to destroy and cast aside this most crucial element. This is a characteristic of devilish functions, known as "robbers of life."

To reject the oneness of mentor and disciple is to reject the mutual possession of the Ten Worlds; it constitutes an attack on the fundamental equality of all human beings. The true nature of the Nikken sect is revealed here for all to see.

The sixty-fifth high priest, Nichijun, clearly recognized the mentor-disciple relationship as the cornerstone of faith in the Soka Gakkai. In the original text of the speech he prepared for the Nineteenth Soka Gakkai General Meeting in November 1958, he writes: "The Daishonin said, 'Nichiren's teaching represents the third doctrine'⁵ (WND, 855). President Toda truly embraced this teaching with his life. The path of mentor and disciple originates from the Dai-Gohonzon and it is my belief that the water of that teaching has run down to the present, now flowing through the Soka Gakkai."

Suda: This is a very important statement. Concerning the distinction between the path of mentor and disciple and the path of the oneness of mentor and disciple, I will never forget a section in your narrative history *The Human Revolution* where the unified struggle of President Toda and Shin'ichi Yamamoto is eloquently described.

It reads:

> Toda dearly wanted to produce many capable leaders from under his wing, but the time was not yet ripe. His disciples understood the way of mentor and disciple, but almost none of them truly grasped how vital the oneness of mentor and disciple was in the struggle for kosen-rufu. Oneness meant a perfect unity or fusion.

When the 1956 election campaign approached, Toda's disciples turned to him for guidance. But having already formulated a course of action in their minds based on conventional wisdom, they merely listened to Toda's basic guidelines as a theoretical framework; they only comprehended them as a point of reference for their own strategies. Strictly speaking, their plans departed from Toda's guidance. This tells us that it is easy to follow the path of mentor and disciple but extremely difficult to follow the path of the oneness of mentor and disciple....

There was, however, one exception—Shin'ichi Yamamoto.... His plans accorded exactly with Toda's guidelines in every particular. They were one and the same. He no longer had to try to understand Toda's guidance; it was automatic and effortless.... For Shin'ichi, everything started from his oneness with Toda—the oneness in the depths of their minds.[6]

Saito: The path of the oneness of mentor and disciple means to stand up and fight with the same mind and the same prayer as the mentor.

Ikeda: The mutual possession of the Ten Worlds expounded in the Lotus Sutra is the fundamental principle that enables all people to transform their state of life. We must manifest this principle in our own lives and pass it on to posterity, on into the infinite future. This golden path is the way of the oneness of mentor and disciple.

In a broader sense, no important undertaking, no movement, nothing of truly great import can be completed in a single generation. Having successors to inherit and continue the task through future generations is vital. I said as much to President Nelson Mandela of South Africa at our first meeting in 1990: "Though your country has in you an unprecedented and great leader, unless there are many excellent people behind you, your job will never be accomplished. One tall tree does not make a jungle." And at our 1995 meeting, when I asked him about his successors, President Mandela confidently assured me that there was no need to worry on that score.

Nichiren Daishonin writes on the importance of successors: "No one was found there who could embrace these sutras and teach them to others. It was as though there were only wooden or stone statues garbed in priests' robes and carrying begging bowls" (WND, 401).

When the Bodhisattvas of the Earth make their appearance in the "Emerging from the Earth" chapter, Shakyamuni announces that these bodhisattvas have been together with their mentor from the beginningless past; they have been inseparable in age after age. Just before he makes this announcement, he declares: "'The Thus Come One wishes now to summon forth and declare...the power of the Buddhas that has the lion's ferocity,...'" (LS15, 218).

Nichiren Daishonin also describes the determination with which he inscribed the Gohonzon as "the power [of the Buddhas] that has the lion's ferocity" (WND, 412). And in reference to his actual inscription of the Gohonzon—the means by which all living beings in the ten thousand years and more of the Latter Day of the Law can attain enlightenment—he proclaims, "I, Nichiren, have inscribed my life in sumi ink"[7] (WND, 412).

The impassioned spirit to fight for the people, for humanity through all eternity—this is the power of an attacking lion; it is the unstinting efforts the mentor makes to educate and train the disciples.

The Lotus Sutra calls out for the mentor and the disciples to work together with the power of a lion's ferocity, unified in heart, mind and purpose, to transform the inner state of life of all humanity.

NOTES

1. John Donne, *Devotions*, XVII, (1624). Editor's note: Spelling and punctuation have been modernized.

2. *Kanjin no Honzon Sho Mondan* (Commentary on the "True Object of Worship"), p. 676.

3. Ibid., p. 548.

4. Fyodor Dostoevsky, *A Raw Youth*, trans. Constance Garnett (New York: The Macmillan Company, 1950), p. 56.

5. The third doctrine: Refers to the comparison of the Buddhism of the harvest and the Buddhism of sowing—the third level of comparison of the threefold secret teaching—specifically indicating the supreme teaching hidden in the depths of the "Life Span" chapter of the Lotus Sutra. Nichiren Daishonin revealed this teaching for the first time as Nam-myoho-renge-kyo, the seed for the direct attainment of Buddhahood.

6. From the chapter "Determination," *The Human Revolution*, vol. 10.

7. Sumi: Black Chinese ink.

8 The Heart of the True Aspect of All Phenomena: The Endless Challenge To Transform Reality

Saito: A member who has been active in our movement since the early days of the Soka Gakkai told me about a little-known period when you, President Ikeda, were writing your lectures on Nichiren Daishonin's thesis "The Selection of the Time" back in the early 1960s. While consulting closely with top leaders of the Study Department, you dedicated yourself to understanding and explaining each word and phrase of that work. This member said he had the opportunity to witness firsthand the ardent commitment with which you gave yourself to this task.

Endo: "The Selection of the Time" is a very important writing in that it prophesies the future accomplishment of worldwide kosen-rufu. Nichiren Daishonin proclaims that at that time—when the age of kosen-rufu arrives—people the world over will chant Nam-myoho-renge-kyo together.

Saito: A passage in the same section where the Daishonin makes this assertion reads: "Great struggles and disputes such as have never been known in the past will break out in the Jambudvipa" (WND, 542). Those who have not awakened to the True Law, the Daishonin tells us, will persecute and slander the practitioners of the Lotus Sutra, and great conflicts of unprecedented scope and magnitude will occur throughout the world.

According to my friend, the Study Department leaders with

whom you were discussing this work, President Ikeda, apparently suggested that this particular passage could be interpreted as predicting the occurrence of World War III. Seeing that it was right in the middle of the Cold War and an escalating nuclear arms race, many people feared that such a global war was in the wings.

But you adamantly rejected this conclusion. "If World War III were to occur," you said with some vehemence, "the entire human race would be wiped out by nuclear weapons. Must humanity be subjected to even crueler and more horrible suffering than it already has? To allow this to happen would show an abominable lack of compassion as a Buddhist! Let us decide right now that it is World War II to which the Daishonin refers when he speaks of 'great struggles and disputes such as have never been known in the past.' Whatever happens, we cannot permit another world war to occur. Let us pray to the Gohonzon with strong determination to prevent such a thing at all costs, pledging to dedicate our lives ungrudgingly to the cause of propagating the Law. Let us definitely achieve kosen-rufu — the dream of lasting peace and happiness for all humanity!"

My friend was very moved by what you said. He remarked to me: "Many religions preach Armageddon or some apocalyptic end of the world. They irresponsibly arouse feelings of anxiety in people, and some of the leaders and practitioners of these religions even come to yearn for the world to end. President Ikeda firmly declared that Nichiren Daishonin's Buddhism is the exact opposite of such religions."

Ikeda: The Daishonin's Buddhism is first and last a Buddhism of peace. Nichiren Daishonin sought to bring peace to the entire world. Hence his adamant insistence on establishing the True Law and propagating the Lotus Sutra so that this goal of peace for all humanity could in fact be realized.

The Daishonin was utterly convinced we could change even the most dire and painful reality, including the danger of war, and, indeed, that it was imperative we do so. This conviction underlies his unwavering determination to create a peaceful society by widely disseminating the teachings of Buddhism.

The SGI has inherited this spirit and is taking positive action for the happiness of all humankind. Fifty years ago, the second Soka Gakkai president, Josei Toda, stood alone amid the devastation wrought by war and declared: "I don't want to see the Japanese people plunged into greater depths of suffering than they have experienced so far.... Who will save, who will help, this suffering world? Now is precisely the time to widely spread Nichiren Daishonin's teachings—the time to carry out kosen-rufu."

"Expedient Means," the second chapter of the Lotus Sutra, which we will continue to discuss in this chapter, teaches the principle of the true aspect, or entity, of all phenomena.[1] In fact, the true aspect of all phenomena provides the theoretical basis for the principle of transforming reality. Shall we discuss this at length today?

Saito: Let's start by examining how the true entity of all phenomena is explained in "Expedient Means."

> "But stop, Shariputra, I will say no more. Why? Because what the Buddha has achieved is the rarest and most difficult-to-understand Law. The true entity of all phenomena can only be understood and shared between Buddhas. This reality consists of the appearance, nature, entity, power, influence, inherent cause, relation, latent effect, manifest effect, and their consistency from beginning to end." (LS2, 24)

> *(Shi shari-hotsu. Fu shu bu setsu. Sho-i sha ga. Bussho joju. Dai ichi ke-u. Nange shi ho. Yui butsu yo butsu. Nai no kujin. Shoho jisso. Sho-i shoho. Nyo ze so. Nyo ze sho. Nyo ze tai. Nyo ze riki. Nyo ze sa. Nyo ze in. Nyo ze en. Nyo ze ka. Nyo ze ho. Nyo ze honmakkukyo to.)*

Suda: The passage in question is one we recite during morning and evening gongyo.

Saito: Before and after this passage, the sutra repeatedly emphasizes how wonderful and difficult it is to understand the wisdom of the Buddhas. Here it states explicitly that the Buddha wisdom constitutes a complete insight and understanding of the true aspect of all phenomena. And it explains what that true aspect is in terms of the ten factors of life: appearance, nature, entity, power, influence, internal cause, relation, latent effect, manifest effect and their consistency from beginning to end.

Suda: In the previous chapter, we discussed the replacement of the three vehicles—the vehicles of the voice-hearers, *pratyekabuddhas* and bodhisattvas—with the one Buddha vehicle. According to the Great Teacher T'ien-t'ai of China, this part of the sutra where the true entity of all phenomena and the ten factors are expounded is a presentation of the "concise" replacement of the three vehicles with the one vehicle, because the idea is presented here in an abbreviated form.

Ikeda: The Buddha appeared in the world to lead people of all backgrounds and circumstances to enlightenment. The Buddha taught that attaining Buddhahood is the most fundamental goal of life; all other aspirations are of a far lesser dimension, functioning merely as expedient means. It is obvious then just how unsuitable fame and fortune are as goals of human life.

The replacement of the three vehicles with the one Buddha vehicle, meanwhile, is a revelation of both the Buddha's true intent and the true purpose of human life. But since this section presents it only in an abbreviated form, the replacement of the three vehicles with the one vehicle is at this point only "dimly" revealed. The Daishonin likened this to a person just awakening from sleep who, still drowsy, hears the first cry of the cuckoo. The cuckoo did cry, but the person isn't really sure of having heard it or not (see WND, 249). That's just how difficult this revelation is to grasp.

Nevertheless, there is no mistaking that the Buddha did in fact reveal his true intent here. The Daishonin writes: "In the 'Expedient Means' chapter of the Lotus Sutra, in the section that concisely reveals the replacement of the three vehicles with the one vehicle, the Buddha briefly explained the concept of three thousand realms in a single moment of life, the doctrine that he had kept in mind for his final revelation" (WND, 249).

And, from another writing: "The basis for the [Lotus Sutra's] assertion that all living beings can enter the Buddha way is found nowhere but in the phrase 'the true aspect of all phenomena'" (GZ, 1139).

Suda: How is it possible that this short expression "the true entity of all phenomena" can constitute the basis for the enlightenment of all living beings? This is the difficult part, isn't it?

Endo: I'll start by examining the most basic meaning of the expression. "All phenomena" means all forms and events here in our actual world. And "true entity" means, just as the words imply, the truth. In his *Profound Meaning of the Lotus Sutra*, T'ien-t'ai interprets "entity" to indicate something indestructible in essence that, while not visible, Buddhas can clearly apprehend.

Ikeda: It is not visible but nevertheless definitely exists.

Saito: Yes. So the ten factors of life are another way of expressing this truth which, though not visible to the eye, indisputably exists.

The Chinese characters representing the term *factor (nyoze)* in this doctrine carry the meaning of "as it is." So the Buddha proclaims in the sutra that he has grasped and understood the true entity of all events and individual lives (all phenomena), describing them as: appearance as it is *(nyoze so)*, nature as it is *(nyoze sho)*, entity as it is *(nyoze tai)*, and so forth.

Ikeda: Yes. The Buddha's revelation of the true entity of all phenomena is very important. The truth (true entity) of things is not found in some far distant realm removed from reality. In this unwavering focus on the true form (true entity) of everyday reality, never moving away from real things and events (all phenomena), we can discern the true brilliance of the Buddha's wisdom.

The "Life Span" chapter says: "'The Thus Come One perceives the true aspect of the threefold world exactly as it is…'" (LS16, 226). The "threefold world" is the world of reality. The Buddha is determined never to become alienated or divorced from the actual world (all phenomena). At the same time, the Buddha is not influenced by the superficial appearance of the actual world (all phenomena) but instead grasps the supreme truth (true entity) concealed therein and teaches it to others so that they may understand and apply it in their own lives. This is the wisdom of Buddhism.

The expression "the true entity of all phenomena" brims with thoroughgoing realism and wisdom for surmounting our immediate circumstances that are both so characteristic of Buddhism.

Suda: Yes, that is very clear. Let us look a little more closely at the ten factors of life. "Appearance" is the external appearance or form of things. "Nature" is the inherent nature, disposition or potential of a thing, not visible from the outside. According to T'ien-t'ai, the ultimate form of nature is the Buddha nature. "Entity" is that which manifests itself as appearance and nature. Together, appearance, nature and entity are known as the three factors of life. They explain the reality of all phenomena, each individual life, from three perspectives.

Saito: These three factors allow each individual life to be viewed as an integrated whole. As a result, they have been linked to and also used as the basis for many other Buddhist doctrines such as the three truths (nonsubstantiality, temporary existence and the

Middle Way) and the three bodies of the Buddha (the Dharma body, the bliss body and the manifested body).

Suda: To continue, "power" refers to the latent potential of life. "Influence" is that power manifesting in life. "Inherent cause" refers to the internal causes of change that each individual phenomenon possesses, while "relation" refers to conditions both internal and external and to indirect causes that prompt change to occur. "Latent effect" is the direct effect of any change, and "manifest effect" is the perceptible manifestation of the latent effect. The four factors of inherent cause, relation, latent effect and manifest effect fall under the general category of "cause and effect."

Saito: The Great Teacher Miao-lo of China writes: "Without a discussion of the ten factors of life, the principle of cause and effect could not exist."[2] He sees the function of cause and effect as the distinctive characteristic of the ten factors of life.

Ikeda: Yes. Cause and effect are important, especially as they relate to our attainment of enlightenment, that is, whether we can actually become Buddhas.

Nichiren Daishonin describes the ten factors of life as "the cause and effect of the material and spiritual aspects of life" (GZ, 239). Each entity of life (all phenomena) possesses the two aspects of cause and effect in both the spiritual and material aspects of being and continually undergoes an endless variety of changes. The Buddha perceived this true entity of life just as it is.

Endo: The last of the ten factors, "consistency from beginning to end," means that all of the preceding nine factors—beginning with "appearance" and ending with "manifest effect"—are consistent and coherent throughout. In other words, the state of Hell is whole and internally consistent, just as the world of Buddhahood is whole and internally consistent.

Ikeda: And the eye of the Buddha perceives that true reality. The true reality (true entity) of all phenomena is that each possesses latent potential (nature and power) and an openness to change (internal cause, relation, latent effect and manifest effect). Moreover, each phenomenon is a self-consistent whole. Phenomena depend upon each other, are open to each other, yet remain consistent and unified. Though I won't go into the details now, this outlook can also be seen in the doctrines of dependent origination and the three truths.

Suda: In "The True Aspect of All Phenomena," Nichiren Daishonin writes: "Hell's displaying the form of hell is its true aspect. When hell changes into the realm of hungry spirits, that is no longer the true form of hell" (WND, 384).

Ikeda: The factor of "consistency from beginning to end" can be viewed from a higher plane as well. Namely, that in terms of the true entity to which the Buddha became enlightened, the life of the Buddha (beginning) and the lives of beings in the nine worlds (end) are ultimately equal (consistent) as entities of the Mystic Law. Hence, all living beings can become Buddhas once they awaken to the true reality of their own lives—that is, that they themselves are entities of the Mystic Law. Ignorance or awareness of this truth is the only difference between a Buddha and persons of the nine worlds. Nichiren Daishonin states:

> "Beginning" refers to the Buddha nature, while "end" refers to the not-yet-manifested Buddhas, the living beings of the nine worlds. "Consistency" indicates that the Thus Come One who has attained the ultimate stage of perfect enlightenment and we ordinary people who are ignorant of our own Buddha nature are ultimately equal and without distinction. This is the meaning of "consistency" and the reason the Lotus Sutra is acclaimed for its great impartial wisdom. (GZ, 413)

Endo: I am gradually coming to understand the meaning of the Daishonin's statement that the principle of the true entity of all phenomena is the basis of enlightenment for all living beings. The true entity of all phenomena means that though there are various differences and distinctions among phenomena, as far as their true entity is concerned they are all equally entities of the Mystic Law.

Ikeda: Yes. "True aspect" refers to the true reality of life as viewed from the enlightened state of the Buddha, who has broken free of all delusion. Here, all things are equal, transcending distinctions and differences between subject and object, self and others, mind and body, the spiritual and the material. In its true aspect of life it is infinitely expansive and eternal, without beginning or end and transcending distinctions of the Ten Worlds.

Life is dynamic; it is wisdom and compassion; it embodies the principle of the indivisibility of life and death; it is a universal law. The cosmos is not so big that life cannot embrace it, nor a particle of matter so small that life cannot be contained within it. It transcends words and thought and is truly unfathomable; it can only be described as the Mystic Law. That is how inscrutable it is.

Shakyamuni became enlightened to the fact that this aspect of life was the true aspect of the lives of all living beings of the Ten Worlds (all phenomena), thus awaking to the true entity of all phenomena (the Ten Worlds).

Hence, the Daishonin writes: "It [this sutra passage] means that all beings and environments in the Ten Worlds, from hell, the lowest, to Buddhahood, the highest, are without exception manifestations of Myoho-renge-kyo" (WND, 383).

Though infinite in number, all phenomena are a part of "all beings and environments in the Ten Worlds." To view all of them, without exception, as equal manifestations of Myoho-renge-kyo (consistency from beginning to end) is to see their true entity.

The principle of the ten factors of life tries to illuminate the same truth. The Daishonin writes: "These ten factors of life are Myoho-renge-kyo" (GZ, 415). Elsewhere he states: "Thus, the entire realm of phenomena is no different than the five characters of Myoho-renge-kyo" (WND, 383). My mentor, Josei Toda, also asserted: "The life of the universe is itself Nam-myoho-renge-kyo."[3]

When we clearly perceive the true entity of all phenomena, everything manifests Myoho-renge-kyo: people and plants, the sun and the moon, everything is Myoho-renge-kyo. All phenomena in the universe pulse with the rhythm of Myoho-renge-kyo.

Perhaps we can explain this best in contemporary terms by saying that "all phenomena" refers to all individual lives, while "true entity" constitutes one great cosmic life force. Each of these infinite lives, governed by the cause and effect of the material and spiritual aspects of life, plays an infinitely diverse melody. It may seem superficially as if each plays its own random and independent melody, but that is only a partial view. In fact, the truth is that each melody combines to perform in a single great symphony called the Mystic Law. While each individual melody has its own internal consistency and is whole and complete on its own terms, each also is an indispensable part of the great symphony of cosmic life known as the Mystic Law.

I am speaking metaphorically, of course.

The important thing is that even living beings in Hell, for instance, can become one with the brilliant, shimmering life of the universe itself, once they awaken to the true nature of their beings (their true entity), once they truly come to know themselves. Moreover, this vast cosmic life force can be tapped only in the reality of the individual's own life — even if that reality happens to be the world of Hell.

Where and when is the eternal true aspect of life to be found? It is now; it is here. Enlightened to this truth, one is a Buddha; ignorant of it, one dwells in the nine worlds. Consequently, the world of Bodhisattva is not necessarily close to the world of Buddhahood nor the world of Hell far from it. All living beings in any of the nine worlds can equally manifest the state of Buddhahood within their lives just as they are. Each individual life (all phenomena) is one with the cosmic life (true entity). Nor does this cosmic life (true entity) exist separately from each individual life (all phenomena).

In "The Gift of Rice," Nichiren Daishonin expressed this true aspect of all phenomena as follows: "[The Lotus Sutra] teaches that the mind itself is the great earth, and that the great earth is the grasses and trees" (WND, 1126). "Mind" here is equivalent to the cosmic life.

The pre-Lotus Sutra teachings, representing a still-shallow and provisional body of philosophy, expounded that all phenomena (individual life) derived from the mind (cosmic life). In this case, the mind is like the earth, while all phenomena are like the plants growing in it. According to this paradigm, the mind and phenomena are separate entities.

But the Lotus Sutra teaches something different. The mind *is* the earth and the earth *is* the plants that grow in it. The true entity and all phenomena are one and the same thing. They cannot be divided. The moon and the flowers, each and every thing, are one with the totality of the life of the universe itself.

In the same writing, the Daishonin states: "The meaning of the earlier sutras is that clarity of mind is like the moon, and that purity of mind is like a flower. But it is not so with the Lotus Sutra. It is the teaching that the moon itself is mind, and the flower itself is mind" (WND, 1126).

Saito: Many philosophies attempt to find the truth somewhere beyond phenomena or postulate some fundamental existence that rests beneath all phenomena, but the Lotus Sutra is different, isn't it? "The Gift of Rice," which you just quoted, also contains the very famous statement: "The true path lies in the affairs of this world" (WND, 1126).

Only in the actuality of the "affairs of this world" (all phenomena) can we demonstrate the "true path"—that is, the wisdom of the true entity.

Endo: The "Benefits of the Teacher of the Law" chapter states that those who uphold the sutra will enjoy the benefit of purifying their six sense organs (eye, ear, nose, tongue, body and mind).

With regard to the "mind benefits" of upholding the sutra, it says:

> "The doctrines that [good men and good women who accept the Lotus Sutra] preach…will conform to the gist of the principles and will never be contrary to true reality.
>
> "If they should expound some text of the secular world or speak on matters of government or those relating to wealth or livelihood, they will in all cases conform to the correct Law. (LS19, 263)

T'ien-t'ai commented on this passage:"No worldly affairs of life or work are ever contrary to the true reality [true entity]" (WND, 1126).

Ikeda: This is an example of the immense benefit of the Lotus Sutra. It is a model of behavior for those who embrace its teachings.

Those who have faith in the Lotus Sutra must articulate the truth with a clear recognition of right and wrong, good and evil. Only then will one's actions never in any way be "contrary to the true reality."

Endo: There is an old Chinese saying, "A single fallen leaf signals the arrival of autumn." Seeing a single leaf fall, we may know that autumn is here. We might call the falling leaf "all phenomena" and autumn its "true entity."

Ikeda: The autumn that we cannot see (true entity) reveals itself in the single falling leaf (all phenomena) that we do see. All phenomena are manifestations of the true entity. At the same time, the true entity is manifested in all phenomena.

Suda: I think we can also say that many people possess at least some aspect of the wisdom—albeit it perhaps in an incomplete and fragmentary form—that perceives the true entity within all phenomena. I am referring to people such as scholars and artists, or those who excel in business, or wise mothers who run their households with great efficiency and skill, and so on.

Ikeda: Of course. Even one who does not possess the eye of the Law or the eye of the Buddha may possess the eye of wisdom or the divine eye.

I was constantly amazed at how keen President Toda's mind was. He was a genius at discerning the essence of phenomena. One would be hard pressed to find a leader to rival him.

Looking at Japan's defeat and accompanying devastation in World War II (all phenomena), Mr. Toda declared that it presented a marvelous opportunity for the unprecedented rise of the Daishonin's Buddhism. This, I believe, is a perfect example of the wisdom of the true entity of all phenomena. Also, Mr. Toda wrote in his 1958 New Year's message, a few short months before he died: "The realms of government, labor, culture, the economy, education and many other areas of human endeavor are all showing signs of 'internal strife,' wallowing in the mud of an evil age stained with the five impurities.[4] But it occurs not to one person that this situation represents general punishment for being a nation of people who slandered the Law."[5]

Endo: To what, specifically, was Mr. Toda referring when he used the term *internal strife?*

Ikeda: In the political sphere, the government was split internally over the formation of a new cabinet and ministry appointments. In the workplace, labor union leaders had become alienated from their members. In the cultural domain, various academic factions were warring among themselves, obstructing the creation of a healthy social culture. Mr. Toda was referring to these and similar events.

Suda: We still see these same tendencies today. The problem, as I see it, is why this happens.

Ikeda: Yes. Mr. Toda observed: "Government systems and social institutions were not created to compete and struggle among themselves. They were conceived and adopted to improve the welfare of humanity."[6]

Saito: How true that is!

Ikeda: And he concluded: "The reason that today they have exactly the opposite effect than was intended is that our entire nation opposes the True Law, persecutes those who preach it and commits the offense of slandering the Law. In other words, it is because the people of this country have rejected Nichiren Daishonin's teaching of creating a peaceful society based on the True Law.[7]

Endo: In his treatise "On Establishing the Correct Teaching for the Peace of the Land," the Daishonin offers us a warning, referring to passages from the sutras. He tells us that when the philosophy and religion upon which people base their lives become distorted and confused, and if this situation continues without people awakening to the True Law, that distortion will without fail be reflected in the nation and society.

Ikeda: When philosophy and religion fall into error and disarray, it means that people's wisdom has become confused and distorted. It then becomes impossible for them to see the true entity of all phenomena, with the result that life itself falls into disarray as well.

Because of the true entity of the oneness of life and its environment, chaos and disharmony in life create corresponding disorder and discord in the environment — that is, in society and the nation.

Suda: As in the three calamities and seven disasters.[8]

Ikeda: In the Daishonin's day, we see a succession of ever more severe disasters taking place. First, there were many different natural disasters. Then there were uprisings caused by political power struggles (the disaster of internal strife). Finally, Japan faced the greatest disaster of all, foreign invasion, when the Mongol forces attacked.

Centuries later, Mr. Toda stated: "Now that we have entered the age of kosen-rufu, disasters are occurring in an order opposite of their appearance during the Daishonin's lifetime." In other words, Japan first experienced the ultimate disaster of invasion from abroad with its defeat in World War II. This was followed by internal conflict as seen in the subsequent schisms and rivalries in every area of society.

The only way to cure the malaise caused by rejecting the Mystic Law is to return to it. That is why Mr. Toda so adamantly proclaimed that widely disseminating the Mystic Law was the only means to bring happiness to all.

Saito: With his profound knowledge of the sutras and the Daishonin's writings, Mr. Toda was deeply concerned about the future of the Japanese people. He keenly apprehended the true entity of all phenomena with regard to postwar Japanese society.

Ikeda: As an example of his prescience, he would often cite the development of improved transportation as one clear sign (all phenomena) that the great development of the kosen-rufu movement was assured. He said it was truly a wonderful thing that large numbers of people could gather together. And it has turned out just as he predicted.

In any case, the true entity of all phenomena is fundamentally a principle of transforming the present. We do not seek to remove ourselves from reality, full as it is of sufferings. We do not try to escape it. The true entity of all phenomena is the wisdom that enables people to bring forth the state of Buddhahood within their lives, to realize a world where peace and tranquillity prevail within the reality of everyday existence.

Endo: We could perhaps say that realizing the true entity of all phenomena is, on the individual level, the attainment of Buddhahood in this lifetime, and on the level of society as a whole, the achievement of a peaceful society through the teachings of Buddhism.

Ikeda: That's precisely right. The attainment of Buddhahood in this lifetime means to achieve enlightenment within this actual world and this life.

We speak of attaining Buddhahood, but it is not something that implies a fixed or static goal, like the finishing line in a race. It means struggling in the midst of reality and bringing forth the state of Buddhahood in our own lives just as we are.

The world of Buddhahood is found nowhere but in the strong mind of faith that seeks always to advance from the state of suffering to the state of Buddhahood and to then proceed from that state of Buddhahood to transform reality. It is the strength and determination of faith to keep on fighting.

In "The Object of Devotion for Observing the Mind," the Daishonin writes: "That ordinary people born in the latter age can believe in the Lotus Sutra is due to the fact that the world of Buddhahood is present in the human world" (WND, 358).

Suda: The twenty-sixth high priest, Nichikan, also writes: "Strong faith in the Lotus Sutra is called the world of Buddhahood."[9] This means that the true entity of all phenomena can be realized through faith. This is a major difference from T'ien-t'ai's teaching.

Ikeda: Yes. T'ien-t'ai's method of realizing the true entity of all phenomena is called 'the threefold contemplation in a single mind.' It is a practice of contemplating the profound principle of the true entity of all phenomena and striving to attain a clear experience of it.

The practice consists mainly of meditation. But it is a difficult method, and not everyone can perform the practice effectively.

Most people, for instance, set free in a dense forest without an accurate compass or map, will lose their direction; very few will find their way out and reach their destination.

What, in contrast, is the practice of Nichiren Daishonin's Buddhism? In the Gosho, he writes: "Both the principle of three thousand realms in a single moment of life and the practice of the threefold contemplation in a single mind are included in the five characters of Myoho-renge-kyo. Similarly, the five characters of Myoho-renge-kyo are contained within our lives" (GZ, 414).

In another Gosho, he also writes: "This great mandala is the essence of the doctrine of three thousand realms in a single moment of life" (GZ, 1339).

A "single moment of life" refers to the true entity and the "three thousand realms" represents all phenomena. The Gohonzon is the Gohonzon of the true entity of all phenomena, a mirror in which the true entity of all phenomena of all living beings is reflected.

The inscription down the center of the Gohonzon, "Nam-myoho-renge-kyo, Nichiren," is an expression of the true entity, and the characters for the Ten Worlds written to its right and left represent all phenomena. The voice of the Mystic Law we produce as we chant daimoku to this Gohonzon of the true entity of all phenomena calls up the Buddha nature within us.

Once summoned, the Buddha nature seeks to manifest itself externally. Consequently, whether we are aware of it or not, the brilliant sun of the ten factors of life of the world of Buddhahood rises in our hearts. The clear blue sky of inherent and eternal being fills the inner expanse of our lives.

When we chant Nam-myoho-renge-kyo with faith in the Gohonzon, we ourselves (all phenomena) shine as entities of the Mystic Law (true entity). This is truly a method for attaining Buddhahood in this lifetime that is accessible to all individuals.

The Gohonzon outside us is Myoho-renge-kyo; our lives within are Myoho-renge-kyo. Our faith in the Gohonzon at the same time is the wisdom to grasp the true entity of all phenomena of our own lives. This is the principle of substituting faith for wisdom.

Suda: In "On Attaining Buddhahood," the Daishonin writes: "Therefore, when you chant myoho and recite renge, you must summon up deep faith that Myoho-renge-kyo is your life itself" (WND, 3). He is saying, in short, that our own lives (all phenomena) are identical to Myoho-renge-kyo (true entity).

Saito: The Daishonin also states:

> Since our essential nature is Myoho-renge-kyo, Myoho-renge-kyo is not simply the name of the sutra [the Lotus Sutra]. Once we awaken to the fact that the Lotus Sutra is our own being, our lives instantaneously become the Lotus Sutra. Because the Lotus Sutra represents the words of the Buddha who summoned forth and revealed to us the essence of our own being, we ourselves become the Thus Come One of original enlightenment who possesses the three bodies in one.[10] (GZ, 411)

Here, the Daishonin stresses that it is a fallacy to believe that Myoho-renge-kyo, or the Lotus Sutra, is simply a sutra title; indeed, it is our very selves. He indicates that it constitutes the words uttered by the Buddha to call forth our original nature (our true entity).

Suda: How are we changed when we grasp this fact from the depths of our lives? The following passage further elucidates this: "Once we realize this, the delusions that we have been under the spell of since the beginningless past to the present disappear completely like yesterday's dream" (GZ, 411).

In other words, the misguided belief or delusion that we are nothing but a small and insignificant existence disappears without a trace like last night's dream.

Endo: It is as if, the Daishonin says, clouds that had obscured the moon clear away and the bright orb shines forth (GZ, 414). Once we understand the true entity of all phenomena, we see that the Buddha and living beings are in fact a single, not separate, existence.

But what does this actually mean in terms of our daily lives? Unless we understand that, the true entity of all phenomena remains an empty concept.

Ikeda: Mr. Toda instructed us on this point in an easily intelligible manner:

As a result of embracing the Gohonzon, the life of one who is ill, for example, will be transformed into one of complete peace of mind. Because of this deep, underlying sense of serenity, one will find pleasure in the simple act of living.

Nevertheless, for all that we may enjoy life, we still possess the nine worlds. Therefore, it is inevitable that we will sometimes experience sufferings or problems. But we may find that the nature of our sufferings and problems has changed, too. Whereas before we may have been caught up in our own problems and worries, we now also come to feel concern for others. Don't you think that finding life itself an absolute joy is what it means to be a Buddha?[11]

Life has its pleasures and its pains. But if one has deep faith, all these different phenomena will function to strengthen the ten factors of life of the world of Buddhahood. We can attain a state of life where we can thoroughly enjoy good times and bad. This drives home again just how momentous and unprecedented it was for the Daishonin to reveal the Gohonzon of the true entity of all phenomena. My heart is filled with gratitude when I think of it.

Suda: Yes, in the key writings in which Nichiren Daishonin discusses the true entity of all phenomena, he is always urging his followers to place their faith in the Gohonzon and exert themselves diligently in their practice.

Ikeda: You have made a very important point.

Suda: For example, in "The True Aspect of All Phenomena," the Daishonin writes:"Believe in the Gohonzon, the supreme object of devotion in all of Jambudvipa"; and "Exert yourself in the two ways of practice and study" (WND, 386). Further, in "The Real Aspect of the Gohonzon," he writes:"What is most important is that, by chanting Nam-myoho-renge-kyo alone, you can attain Buddhahood. It will no doubt depend on the strength of your faith. To have faith is the basis of Buddhism" (WND, 832).

Ikeda: The basis of the Daishonin's Buddhism is faith; it is to practice according to the Buddha's teachings based on faith.

Saito: The Japanese Tendai school of Buddhism during Nichiren Daishonin's day also based itself on the Lotus Sutra, but it had lost sight of practicing based on faith. The Tendai priests declared:"All beings are originally Buddhas. Given their innate Buddhahood, therefore, any kind of desire is permissible, any reality acceptable."

Ikeda: This represents a distorted interpretation of the true entity of all phenomena. It is the abandonment of practice and a servile capitulation to circumstance.

The true entity of all phenomena does not simply indicate that all phenomena are equivalent to the true entity. It means that all phenomena are the true entity, and the true entity is all phenomena. They are not equal, they are identical, one and the same with no distinction between them. The Daishonin states, "The single character *soku* (is) means Nam-myoho-renge-kyo" (GZ, 732). The term *soku* here expresses life's dynamism — never still, at times manifest, at times dormant, always creative and expanding.

The true entity of all phenomena, it must be remembered, is, after all, the ultimate truth viewed by the Buddha. It is different from the reality that deluded, unenlightened, ordinary beings see. That is why each person must continually strive to approach the realization of the ultimate truth. This is what our Buddhist practice is all about. We must unceasingly strive to overcome our immediate circumstances, forging our way toward the ideal of the true entity of all phenomena. This is how reform is engendered.

If we turn our backs on this challenge and simply hide behind this wonderful principle of the true entity of all phenomena, we will be swamped by reality and grow powerless and apathetic. And that is a very frightening development, because people's apathy becomes a fertile field for those who wish to wield unchecked power. None are easier to control than people who are passive and without motivation. That is because, however cruel reality may be, such people will meekly accept and affirm it without question.

The wisdom of the true entity of all phenomena teaches us otherwise, the way things should be: that it is our duty to reprimand leaders who violate the true path of life. This is clearly evident in the Daishonin's committed actions to uphold the True Law.

Endo: The Tendai school of Buddhism distorted the Lotus Sutra's teaching of 'the unification of the three vehicles within the one Buddha vehicle' and asserted that any teaching, if it was thought to have the least benefit, was truth. "The Pure Land, Shingon and Zen schools of Buddhism are all the Lotus Sutra," they declared. "To believe that is the true practice."

In this connection, the Daishonin writes: "Today the Tendai school speaks of the [Lotus Sutra] teaching of 'the unification of the three vehicles within the one vehicle.' But, having in fact misunderstood this passage, they expound an erroneous interpretation of the original doctrine" (GZ, 1139).

Suda: The Daishonin fought fiercely against such erroneous teachings. He describes the beliefs of the Tendai priests and much of the Japanese populace of the time as follows:

> They believe that since all vehicles are opened up and incorporated in the one vehicle of Buddhahood, no teaching is superior or inferior, shallow or profound,

but all are equal to the Lotus Sutra. Hence the belief that chanting the Nembutsu, embracing the True Word teaching, practicing Zen meditation, or professing and reciting any sutra or the name of any Buddha or bodhisattva equals following the Lotus Sutra. (WND, 392–93)

And then he adds: "But I insist that this is wrong" (WND, 393). We can see that the Daishonin strictly refutes such distorted beliefs.

Ikeda: The arrogance and irresponsibility of such religious teachers, who assert that all religious beliefs are alike and that whichever one an individual follows is just a matter of personal preference, have created the spiritual climate we observe in Japan today.

Saito: That is absolutely true. Such religious leaders shun strictly distinguishing between true and false, the correct and erroneous, and seek only self-preservation by settling for a superficial harmony between viewpoints. They mistake this wishy-washy compromise as tolerance. They meekly go along with circumstances, surrendering themselves to reality.

As a result, they act as pawns of those in power, seeking to suppress the people who would fight against the injustices wrought by the authorities. Or they just stand on the sidelines, silently allowing justice to be violated, aiding and abetting those who would commit wrongdoing. They think they are living their lives very cleverly, but they don't even notice they have been robbed of their autonomy by the diabolical hands of power.

Suda: Nothing demeans people more than such a self-serving practicality that is completely bereft of ideals.

Endo: The teachings of the Pure Land school are at the other extreme from the Tendai teaching of original Buddhahood. They assert that we cannot become Buddhas in this life but must wait until after we die to be reborn in another place where at last we will be happy.

If we can't become happy in this life, what guarantee is there that we will in the next? This teaching leads the individual to conclude there is no point in making any effort in this life, that it is better to die and go to the next world as quickly as possible. This constitutes an escape from reality, a denial of the present.

Saito: And there is a strong tendency among followers of schools such as Zen Buddhism to cut themselves off from the reality of secular life and withdraw into their own closed-off little world.

Ikeda: Let's take a look at how the Daishonin describes the Buddha who has awakened to the true entity of all phenomena in contrast to these teachings. He writes: "In the phrase 'consistency from beginning to end,' 'beginning' indicates the root of evil and the root of good, while 'end' indicates the outcome of evil and the outcome of good. One who is thoroughly awakened to the nature of good and evil from their roots to their branches and leaves is called a Buddha" (WND, 1121).

To distinguish between good and evil in this world and guide others to happiness is to put into practice the wisdom of the true entity of all phenomena.

Further on in the same writing, he continues: "A person of wisdom is not one who practices Buddhism apart from worldly affairs" (WND, 1121). And he indicates that even people living before the introduction of Buddhism, who worked to relieve human suffering, acted as "emissaries of Shakyamuni Buddha," and that their wisdom "contained at heart the wisdom of Buddhism" (WND, 1122).

Here we can see a very broad and expansive, nondogmatic, nonsectarian way of thinking. While some are losing themselves in the world, allowing themselves to be controlled by reality, or, at the other extreme, closing their eyes to the real world, rejecting it and trying to seek refuge in the next life, the Lotus Sutra teaches an entirely different approach.

The Daishonin harshly criticized the teachings of the Tendai, Zen and Pure Land schools of Buddhism, because they had rejected the teaching of the true entity of all phenomena. The true entity of all phenomena expounded in the Lotus Sutra embodies a philosophy that enables the individual to transform reality. It does not teach fatalism or passive resignation. It seeks to develop in us a resilience that will allow us to fend off all such passivity and feelings of powerlessness. It rouses a fighting spirit within us, the determination to try to effect change at all costs. It summons forth in us a spirit of responsibility, so that we continually ask ourselves what we should be doing right now.

Endo: That reminds me of the theme of your work *The Human Revolution*, which you identify as follows: "A great human revolution in just a single individual will help achieve a change in the destiny of a nation, and further, will enable a change in the destiny of all humankind." This is the wisdom of the Lotus Sutra pure and simple and the fundamental spirit of Nichiren Daishonin's Buddhism.

Ikeda: I am Mr. Toda's disciple. That is my most fundamental source of pride. When Mr. Toda was in prison, he read the Lotus Sutra with his entire life. Many other religious leaders have claimed to understand the Lotus Sutra. Some even founded their own schools of religion. But Mr. Toda was different. When newspaper reporters asked him whether he thought he was the Buddha, he replied, "No, I am a fine example of an ordinary human being." He stood up fearlessly in the midst of the storms that raged about him, always warmly supporting the cause of people who were bravely acting out the inspirational drama of transforming lives of despair into lives of shining new hope and new beginnings.

Mr. Toda's life was the epitome of human revolution. With these two words, *human revolution*, Mr. Toda demolished that danger of self-righteousness that can so easily afflict a religion and marvelously combined the supreme wisdom of Buddhism with an unsurpassed way of life for the human being and a superlative path for social prosperity.

Suda: Yes, I think the concept of human revolution perfectly synthesizes the ideas of attaining Buddhahood in this lifetime and of creating a peaceful society by spreading widely the philosophy and ideals of the Daishonin's Buddhism.

Ikeda: Human revolution simultaneously leads to a revolution of society and of our environment. In "The True Aspect of All Phenomena," the Daishonin cites Miao-lo's observation: "Living beings and their environments always manifest Myoho-renge-kyo" (WND, 383).

T'ien-t'ai, too, says that the land also possesses the ten factors of life. Life and its environment are not separate things. They are inseparable. This is the origin of the principle that human revolution means a simultaneous revolution of the land and society.

Viewed through the eyes of the Buddha—that is, from the perspective of the true entity of all phenomena—all phenomena in the universe are one living entity. Happiness for living beings independent of their environment is impossible. Similarly, peace only in terms of the environment independent of living beings is also impossible.

We cannot be truly happy while others remain miserable. Nor is the misery of another that person's alone. The more happiness we bring to others, the happier we ourselves become. As long as one unhappy person remains, our own happiness cannot be complete.

This is the perspective of life from the true entity of all phenomena. That is why the endless challenge to transform reality is the very heart of the true entity of all phenomena.

In his rationale for having written the thesis "On Establishing the Correct Teaching For the Peace of the Land," Nichiren Daishonin states: "I say all this solely for the sake of the nation, for the sake of the Law, for the sake of others, not for my own sake" (WND, 164). However fiercely the Daishonin was persecuted, the flame in his heart for the salvation of others could not be extinguished.

Tsunesaburo Makiguchi, the first president of the Soka Gakkai, inheriting this spirit and deeply committed to the realization of a peaceful society through the wide dissemination of the True Law, died a martyr's death in prison. With this same spirit, Mr. Toda rose up alone from the barren wasteland of defeat after World War II.

In the "Record of the Orally Transmitted Teachings," the Daishonin says: "The essence of the Lotus Sutra is that earthly desires are in themselves enlightenment and that the sufferings of birth and death are in themselves nirvana"; and "The doctrine that a single moment of life contains three thousand realms removes suffering and imparts pleasure" (GZ, 773).

The sole purpose of Buddhism, the sole purpose of the SGI, is to save people from suffering. The SGI is doing its utmost to bring happiness to humanity. It has no other reason for existing.

How praiseworthy are the lives of those who strive toward that goal with the SGI! How noble!

From the perspective of the true entity of all phenomena, the here and now is our true and eternal sphere of activity. It is the actual stage on which we perform our missions. "There is no need," the Daishonin writes, "to leave this place and go elsewhere" (GZ, 781). Even difficult situations, the kind we can only ascribe to our negative karma, are precious, never-to-be-repeated opportunities to fulfill our original mission.

In that respect, those who understand the wisdom of the true entity of all phenomena can transform any kind of karma into a radiantly brilliant mission. When you are absolutely confident of this, you will be filled with hope. Every person and every experience you encounter will become a precious and unique treasure.

The Indian poet Rabindranath Tagore wrote that life is a deeply satisfying experience and that everything in the world is beautiful down to the smallest particle of dust. In his renowned epic poem *Gitanjali* he adopts the voice of a mother thinking of her child:

When I bring to you coloured toys,
my child, I understand why there is
such a play of colours on clouds, on
water, and why flowers are painted in
tints—when I give coloured toys to
you, my child.
When I sing to make you dance I
truly know why there is music in leaves,
and why waves send their chorus of
voices to the heart of the listening
earth—when I sing to make you dance.[11]

A world of brilliant colors glows in the heart of a mother who loves her child. The vibrant rhythm of life echoes within her. This is because love transcends the individuality of life and opens our hearts to the true entity of life, which is one and indivisible.

That being so, how exquisite must be the hues and melodies brimming within our lives, dedicated as they are to enfolding all of humanity in the warm embrace of compassion!

When we firmly believe in the principle of the true entity of all phenomena, the place we are right now becomes the Land of Eternally Tranquil Light, and the very act of living itself becomes an absolute delight.

We will keep on building and spreading this deep, abiding joy of which Mr. Toda spoke. The Lotus Sutra shows us how to live such a bright, optimistic life of infinite challenge.

NOTES

1. The term *shoho jisso* is translated differently in Burton Watson's translation of *The Lotus Sutra* and in *The Writings of Nichiren Daishonin*. Both "true entity of all phenomena" and "true aspect of all phenomena" refer to the same principle. The text will use the terms interchangeably.

2. *Maka Shikan Bugyoden Guketsu* (Annotations on *Great Concentration and Insight*). A detailed commentary on T'ien-t'ai's *Great Concentration and Insight*.

3. *Toda Josei Zenshu* (The Collected Works of Josei Toda) (Tokyo: Seikyo Shimbunsha, 1982,), vol. 2, p. 413.

4. Five impurities: The impurities of the age, desire, living beings, view and life span.

5. *Toda Josei Zenshu*, vol. 3, p. 295.

6. Ibid., p. 297.

7. Ibid.

8. The three calamities and seven disasters: Calamities and disasters described in various sutras. The three calamities refers to the three great calamities—fire, water and wind—that destroy a world at the end of a kalpa; or the three lesser calamities—famine (also known as high grain prices or inflation), warfare and pestilence. Both are described in "A Treasury of Analyses of the Law." The seven disasters include war and natural disasters caused by slander of the Law. They are mentioned in the Buddha of Medicine Sutra, Benevolent King Sutra and other sources. In the Sutra of Yakushi Buddha, they are listed as: (1) pestilence, (2) foreign invasion, (3) internal rebellion, (4) extraordinary changes in the heavens, (5) solar and lunar eclipses, (6) unseasonable storms and typhoons, and (7) drought.

9. From the "Threefold Secret Teaching."

10. Three bodies: The three kinds of body that a Buddha possesses, namely: (1) the Dharma body or body of the Law, which indicates the fundamental truth to which the Buddha is enlightened; (2) the bliss body, which enables the Buddha to perceive the truth; and (3) the manifested body, or the merciful actions of the Buddha to save people and the physical form that the Buddha assumes in this world for that purpose.

11. *Toda Josei Zenshu*, vol. 2, p. 447.

12. Rabindranath Tagore, *Gitanjali* (London: Macmillan and Co., Ltd., 1915), p. 57.

9 "Expedient Means": The Inherent Sanctity of All Existence

But you and the others already know
how the Buddhas, the teachers of the world,
accord with what is appropriate in employing
  expedient means.
You will have no more doubts or perplexities
but, your minds filled with great joy,
will know that you yourselves will attain Buddhahood.
  (LS2, 46)

Saito: In the previous chapter, we confirmed that the principle of the true aspect of all phenomena is the basis for the attainment of Buddhahood by all living things. This time, we would like to explore the contemporary significance of the true aspect of all phenomena from various perspectives.

This teaching reveals to us the wondrous interrelationship of all things, clarifying that all phenomena — in other words, all individual lives — are identical to the true aspect or entity — that is, the life of the universe. Each part is identical to the whole. Today, many different fields of modern science are affirming this same principle — that the whole is not simply a sum of its parts but, in fact, the whole is contained in each of its parts.

Ikeda: That's very true. In fact, viewed from this perspective, it may even be easier for us today to understand the true aspect of all phenomena than it was for our predecessors over the ages.

Endo: Many scientific findings indicate that the whole is included in its parts. Perhaps the most easily understood example of this is the DNA in our cells.

DNA—deoxyribonucleic acid—is the substance that carries the genetic information of an organism and is found in each of its cells. The human body is made up of approximately two hundred kinds of cells, each with its own function. So it would be natural to assume that the DNA of each type of cell is distinct, but in fact the same DNA is found in almost all cells. In other words, every cell of one's body—whether a cell that produces hair on the head or a liver cell—contains the genetic information of the entire body.

Suda: That was the premise of the movie about cloning dinosaurs, *Jurassic Park.* It suggested that one cell recovered from a fossil would be sufficient to recreate an entire extinct creature, such as a dinosaur.

Ikeda: Precisely because each cell in the body contains a full complement of genetic information, it can perform the function appropriate to its location in the body. A hair cell functions as a hair cell, a liver cell as a liver cell. There is harmony within the body as a whole. This is the mystic function of life.

Josei Toda described this harmony of a living being's component parts in their proper place as exemplifying the Great Teacher T'ien-t'ai's assertion: "The Law of all living beings is mystic"[1] (WND, 417).

Saito: The fact that every cell includes all of the body's genetic information has been likened to an enormous library. The information defining the way we laugh, cry, walk, all our physical traits and characteristics, are included in this giant cellular library.

One scientist has said that the information contained in a single cell is equivalent to a thousand five-hundred-page books. If we take the brain itself as a single library, given that it stores all the information we acquire during our lifetime, it has a storage capacity equivalent to some twenty million books.

Ikeda: It is said that the brain will become the greatest frontier of science in the twenty-first century. It is such a vast realm that it could be described as a miniature cosmos, a universe in its own right. Up until now, I believe, brain research has focused largely on the functions of individual parts of the brain.

Suda: Yes. The parts of the brain that process emotion and the parts that distinguish graphic symbols have been identified.

Ikeda: But as brain research proceeds, we are discovering that the brain is not simply a conglomeration of the functions of its parts. For example, the human brain consists of two hemispheres: the left side, which controls intellectual functions, and the right side, which controls creative and artistic activity. But it is surprising that there are fully functioning individuals who lack an entire hemisphere of the brain. For example, there was a young man who was leading a perfectly normal life but was discovered during a routine medical examination to be missing his left cerebral hemisphere.

Since he was lacking the hemisphere that directs intellectual activity and right-body motor functions, one would expect to find him unable to understand language or to control the right side of his body. But this was not the case. His right cerebral hemisphere had taken over the functions of the missing left hemisphere.

Endo: Life is indeed mysterious. There have been many reports of children born with some dysfunction because parts of their brains were missing. As they grew older, however, their brains repaired themselves until, by adulthood, these individuals were functioning completely normally. There are kindergartens that allow such children to be raised in an ordinary environment with other children, providing them with constant stimulation to help them develop. Even children born with only the brain stem and a portion of the frontal lobe, through such positive interaction and stimulation, have learned to play with other children.

Ikeda: That's most interesting. Life is filled with truly unfathomable potential. At last we are coming to see the enormous power it possesses. That is why we must never count anyone out. In particular, we mustn't put boundaries on our own potential. In most cases, our so-called limitations are nothing more than our own decision to limit ourselves.

Saito: Some suggest there is a similarity between this capacity of the brain to rejuvenate itself and the principles of holography. A hologram is a three-dimensional image created by overlapping waves of light. When the film of a hologram is cut into pieces, each piece contains the whole hologram image. It may not be as sharply focused as the original uncut film image, but the full three-dimensional image is visible.

Ikeda: That reminds me of a line from a poem by William Blake: "To see the World in a grain of sand."[2]

Suda: Fractal theory, which has recently received much attention, is another contemporary articulation of the idea that each part includes the whole. Fractal theory originally developed as a part of geometry. It refers to a structure in which component parts and the whole have the same shape, a characteristic known as self-similarity.

Fractal structures can be seen everywhere in the natural world. The branching of airways in the human lung are fractal, because the branching of even the smallest portion thereof is identical to the branching of the whole system. The same phenomenon can be discerned in the branching of the capillaries in the brain; in the way streams branch out from rivers; in the shapes of clouds; and in the way branches are arranged on trees. This similarity of the part and the whole can be found in many natural phenomena that, until now, were thought to follow no set pattern.

Nor are fractal structures restricted to the natural world. It is said they can be observed even in such things as telecommunications errors and social phenomena, such as stock price fluctuations and the distribution of wealth.

Endo: This concept of the part containing the whole can be stated in terms of the principle of the Ten Worlds: Each world (the part) contains all of the Ten Worlds (the whole). In other words, each of the Ten Worlds is a microcosm of its own.

Suda: Yes, that is the principle of the mutual possession of the Ten Worlds. Each individual life contains the Ten Worlds, and at the same time, the life of the universe itself contains the Ten Worlds. During a discussion on the theory of life, Mr. Toda once said:

> Any other planet with the same conditions for life as Earth inspires a human presence. Perhaps "inspires" is not the best way of putting it. What I mean is that, since the entire universe contains the Ten Worlds, on that other planet, a humanlike life form will appear in response to the Ten Worlds. Let us imagine that only dogs or cats live on that planet — even in that case, humanlike qualities will respond within the animal realm, because the Ten Worlds are mutually inclusive. So in a way a humanlike being would exist on that planet.[3]

Saito: Mr. Toda is describing the principle of "mystic response." Since the universe itself is an entity that embodies all of the Ten Worlds, the Ten Worlds within the universe appear in response to the conditions existing on various planets, in response to various causes, or having sensed that the time or some other circumstance is right for their appearance.

The mutual possession of the Ten Worlds, I think, offers valuable insights that may contribute to the theory of evolution and other aspects of the life sciences.

Ikeda: That is a subject that merits future research. From the stand-point of the wisdom of the true aspect of all phenomena, which sees the part as being identical to the whole, every single thing in existence is worthy of supreme reverence, possessing the treasure of the entire universe. The "Expedient Means" chapter restates the principle of the true entity of all phenomena as: "Phenomena are part of an abiding Law, / that the characteristics of the world are constantly abiding" (LS2, 41). The "characteristics of the world" (all phenomena) are the manifestation (true aspect) of the "abid-ing," or ever-present, Mystic Law.

T'ien-t'ai writes, "All things having color or fragrance are man-ifestations of the Middle Way."[4] The expression "all things having color or fragrance" refers to the tiniest bits of matter. Even the smallest things embody the true aspect of the Middle Way — in other words, they embody the life of the universe.

In that respect, it is absolutely clear that nature is not some-thing for human beings to use and exploit as they see fit, solely for their own interests. Both nature and humanity are part and whole of the life of the universe. Nature and humanity are one. To destroy the natural world is to destroy human life as well.

Endo: The principle of the true aspect of all phenomena has a direct bearing on environmental ethics, then.

Ikeda: Yes. In the "Orally Transmitted Teachings," Nichiren Dai-shonin says: "The countless entities in the three thousand worlds, which are undergoing the process of birth, duration, change and extinction, are all in themselves embodiments of [the Thus Come One's] transcendental powers" (GZ, 753).

In other words, all phenomena, ever-changing, appearing and disappearing, are themselves manifestations of the Thus Come One's transcendental powers. Ceaselessly changing though they are, all things in the universe are in fact always present; they are the Middle Way, the true entity, the Thus Come One.

Mr. Toda remarked:

Ultimately, each instant of existence should be called "Thus Come One." Not only our own lives but all things in the universe never cease to change, not even for the briefest instant. They are transformed and transformed again from one moment to the next. Since every single thing is constantly changing, a house as a house, the very house itself, is constantly changing. Time passes, and it turns into clods and dust. The clods as clods, the clods themselves, become dust, and the dust continues to disintegrate as well.

When we see all things for what they are, this is called the principle of temporary existence. And since these phenomena are temporary, they are not real. In that respect, they are nonsubstantial—this is the principle of nonsubstantiality. If we look at each moment as existing just as it is, that is the Middle Way. So the appearance and nature of all things, in their moment-by-moment existence, are the true aspect. Our moment-by-moment existences and lives are also the true aspect, and in that momentary true aspect, all life from the beginningless past is included, as well as all life into the infinite future. This single instant of life contains the effects of all our past lives and the causes for all our future lives. This is the Law of the Lotus, the law of cause and effect.

This single instant of life is the activity of the universe itself, our own lives and actual existence. The activity of the universe from moment to moment is constantly changing and manifests itself as various phenomena, all of which are undergoing a transformation within that activity. This is what we call "transcendental powers." It is not a matter of someone bestowing some kind of power on us. What it means is that the free and unrestricted transformation of all universal phenomena, in response to all other activity therein, represents the true aspect of the universe.[5]

This was Mr. Toda's view of the true aspect of all phenomena. It is not the least bit different from the passages cited earlier from the Lotus Sutra, T'ien-t'ai or Nichiren Daishonin. These are words to ponder and savor.

Endo: In what you have just quoted, it seems as though Mr. Toda is treating matter and the phenomenon of life in the same way, but I'm a little lost as to how to go about explaining this. I know that "all phenomena" includes both matter and life, but we usually think of the two as distinct.

Ikeda: This is an important point. As "all phenomena" indicates, Buddhism's view of matter, too, is not a fixed and unchanging object but a dynamic phenomenon that goes through a cycle of generation and disintegration. In other words, Buddhism views matter from the dimension of the phenomenal as opposed to the purely material. It regards life, too, as a dynamic phenomenon that undergoes a cycle of birth and death.

Usually, it would be considered a mistake to view a phenomenon in the same way we do a material object, that is, as a static and fixed existence. But we cannot say a phenomenon does not exist. It neither exists nor doesn't exist. Yet there are times when it is reasonable to describe a phenomenon as existing and times when it is just as appropriate to describe it as nonexisting. This way of looking at things is called the Middle Way, because it takes a middle path without adhering either to existence or nonexistence. This is the same as "the true aspect" when it is correctly understood just as it is.

Endo: I see. It's easy to understand when we look at reality in terms of its phenomenal and material dimensions. We could probably apply this to the three truths—nonsubstantiality, temporary existence and the Middle Way—of which Mr. Toda often spoke. For example, to look at matter not as something fixed or static (material) but dynamic (phenomenal) in nature would correspond to the truth of nonsubstantiality. Yet, it is also possible to temporarily view matter as static, and this would correspond to the truth of temporary existence. To refrain from adhering to one view or the other, meanwhile, would represent the truth of the Middle Way. T'ien-t'ai described a perfect and fully integrated understanding of the true aspect of all phenomena from all three of these perspectives as the "unification of the three truths." This was the true aspect of all phenomena of which he spoke.

Ikeda: All things reside in the realm of phenomena, subject to the cycle of birth, duration, change and extinction. What we call matter is simply a phenomenon that has entered a temporary stage of stability or duration.

Suda: Classical science, and particularly its core of Newtonian mechanics, is based on a material view of existence. For example, in Newtonian mechanics, two objects exist, and between those two solid objects operates a force called gravity. This system explained many physical phenomena very adroitly. But as an eventual result, life came to be viewed primarily as nothing more than matter, nothing more than a machine.

Ikeda: This view, however, is not really fundamental to science itself.

Endo: No, it is not part of science per se. Its real source is in the "religion" of science, I would say. Some describe this tendency to fix on one aspect of reality and then declare that it applies to everything as "reductionism." This kind of reductionist thinking makes the error of reducing the whole to one of its parts and then extending that partial view to encompass the whole.

Saito: I think this reductionist view has cast a dark shadow over people's lives today and has robbed them of hope and contributed to an increase in their sense of powerlessness.

Ikeda: To avoid the error of worshiping science as a religion, we need a true philosophy that expresses a holistic view of life. Proper scientific method recognizes a partial view as just that—a partial view. And since the search for truth lies at the very root of science, when a once-authoritative partial view reaches a dead end, science strives to break through that impasse and discover new, more creative theories that approach reality more closely. This is how scientific revolutions occur.

Suda: Many of these scientific revolutions, as historical records show, are sparked by one individual's genius and creativity.

Ikeda: Naturally, that is an important factor. Human beings, after all, are wellsprings of creativity. Brilliant scientists like Albert Einstein are a good example, I think.

Josei Toda, incidentally, accompanied Tsunesaburo Makiguchi to a lecture by Einstein when the latter visited Japan in 1922. Mr. Toda later described that occasion as one of the greatest joys of his life.

Einstein described the motivation for his passionate search for the truth as "a cosmic religious feeling."[6] It was, he said, "to experience the universe as a single significant whole." He perceived "the sublimity and marvelous order which reveal themselves both in nature and in the world of thought." He also wrote that "Buddhism...contains a much stronger element of [this cosmic religious feeling]."

Einstein emphasized that science and religion are not in opposition. Not only was religious feeling a motivation for scientific pursuit, but the results of scientific investigation made humankind humble in the face of the wondrous natural laws that govern all existence. He writes:

> This attitude, however, appears to me to be religious, in
> the highest sense of the word. And so it seems to me
> that science not only purifies the religious impulse of

the dross of its anthropomorphism but also contributes to a religious spiritualization of our understanding of life.[7]

The main source of conflict between science and religion, according to Einstein, was the "concept of a personal God."[8] The "dross of anthropomorphism" refers to this concept. The humble search for the law of life, which is the way of Buddhism, was, according to Einstein, simultaneously scientific and religious. From the Buddhist perspective, we could say that Buddhism is an all-encompassing body of wisdom focused on the totality of life, while science is focused on temporary aspects of existence. In that sense, science is a part of Buddhism. That is why there is no conflict between the two. All the truths of the world are, without exception, the Buddhist Law.

Mr. Toda often said that the more science advanced, the more it would demonstrate the validity and truth of the Buddhist teachings. Of course, science and Buddhism belong to two separate dimensions, and their approaches are different as well. I am not saying that Buddhist teachings are correct by virtue of their validation by science. Scientific knowledge changes and evolves daily, but the absolute truths of Buddhism are in no way affected by the relative truths of science.

Nevertheless, we can see that the more science advances, the more it is arriving at a position in harmony with Buddhism. Today, this agreement acts as a strong recommendation of the preeminence of Buddhist philosophy. For example, Einstein's theory of relativity is extremely close to a worldview that is phenomenal (dynamic and integrated) as opposed to material (static and mechanistic), don't you think?

Saito: Yes. The theory of relativity postulates that all physical phenomena exist in a four-dimensional continuum known as space-time, where the three dimensions of space are merged with the dimension of time. In classical Newtonian mechanics, time and space were regarded as absolute and separate. This was based on our everyday perceptions of and assumptions about time—for example, that time passes at the same rate for a person riding in an automobile and a person walking along the road. But the theory of relativity tells us that the faster one is moving through space the slower time passes in relation to how it does for a stationary observer.

Time and space are indivisible, in other words. One cannot be divorced from the other. It is the relationship (phenomenal in nature) between the two that governs the way each of them appears.

Suda: Modern physics has also discovered that it is impossible to accurately measure at the same time the position and velocity of an object, especially in the realm of subatomic particles. The attempt of measurement itself exerts an influence on the activity of these particles. At work here is Heisenberg's uncertainty principle, which effectively destroyed the distinction between object and subject upon which modern analytical science rested. In other words, object and subject are inseparable. The results of scientific observation are determined by the relationship between observer and observed.

Ikeda: In its pursuit of the basic building blocks of the universe—a search taking it to ever smaller components, from molecules to atoms, from atoms to subatomic particles—modern science has stumbled on a paradox; that the most basic subatomic particles have a dual nature. They are not only particles but also waves. This discovery has forced scientists to reassess their way of looking at the world of matter, hitherto viewed as fixed and unchanging, and instead view it in terms of the actual changes occurring to matter itself and the interrelationship among different kinds of matter. In other words, to take a phenomenal, integrated view. They were also compelled to take into account the relationship between observer and object.

The picture of the world painted by modern physics has thus undergone a dramatic change, from a conglomeration of infinite matter to a tapestry of infinite relationships. And this latter vision of the world has much in common with the insights and perceptions of Mahayana Buddhism.

Saito: Einstein revealed that matter is simply energy in a temporarily stable state. According to this theory, matter and energy are not separate. But, at the same time, they always take either one form or the other. In other words, they are indivisible but manifest themselves temporarily as separate.

Einstein discovered that energy equals mass times the speed of light squared. This is the famous equation $E=mc^2$. Light travels at close to 186,000 miles per second; so it is clear that an enormous amount of energy is produced by a tiny amount of mass.

Endo: This discovery was later used in developing the atomic bomb.

Ikeda: Yes, it was a tragedy that Einstein's theory took on a life of its own, employed by people who did not understand the significance of the phenomenal worldview, which the theory originally suggested. The world is an intricately interwoven web of infinite relationships. When we apply this worldview to matter and to all living things, including people, we can see the world as Mr. Toda did, as one great life entity, as the Thus Come One. And further, we can perceive that it is the true aspect of our own existence as well.

A weapon such as the atomic bomb, whose only purpose is destruction and division, is nothing more than a product of the ignorance and delusion that shroud the true aspect of existence. The fundamental darkness inherent in life manifests itself as the devil king of the sixth heaven. Mr. Toda declared that whoever used atomic weapons was a devil incarnate, a fiend. This declaration expressed his enormous rage at anyone who would violate and annihilate life, something so infinitely precious and noble.

At any rate, the revolution in scientific thought from a static to a dynamic worldview shook all human thought to its very foundations. We might say that this scientific revolution, the result of analytical reasoning having reached its limits, has provided us with a glimpse of a vast realm with which a static, partial worldview could not come to grips. It was based on that realization that Einstein and Heisenberg, among others, came to reflect on the existence of a larger whole, the ultimate reality of which the mechanical laws of physics occupied only a portion.

Suda: Analytical reasoning has been a powerful weapon of modern science. Many of the rules governing the natural world were discovered by finely partitioning the material world so that it could be easily observed and reducing the complexities of natural phenomena to simpler elements. In that process of simplifying phenomena into their elements, there is a tendency to discard or ignore other aspects of those phenomena.

Instead of turning their attention to the true aspect inherent in all ever-changing, interrelated phenomena, the inclination is to view such phenomena as fixed entities, ignoring certain aspects of them, and proceed to extract laws from this limited reality — laws that they then regard as the whole truth.

Endo: Recently, there has been reaction within the scientific community to thought of this kind. One such reaction has been the recognition that we have gained only a very limited, partial understanding of the natural world by means of rational analysis.

We see frequent evidence that science cannot predict future events, no matter how deeply it may analyze phenomena. I have no intention whatsoever of criticizing the work of meteorologists, but weather forecasting is the perfect example of this inability to predict the future. Long-term weather forecasts, in fact, are generally expected to be wrong! There are simply too many complex, interrelated meteorological factors to be taken into account for accurate long-term weather forecasts to be possible through any sort of analytical reasoning.

Saito: There has recently appeared a new stream of scientific thought known as the "science of complexity." While science has tried to attain certain knowledge by simplifying phenomena and stripping them of their natural complexity, the science of complexity focuses on the complex nature of phenomena just as it is, without reducing phenomena to simpler models that are easier to analyze. America's Santa Fe Research Institute in New Mexico is famous for its new research system that dismantles the traditional boundaries of biology, mathematics, physics and other sciences and seeks to comprehend phenomena from a holistic perspective.

Suda: Weather, ecology and the brain are all examples of complex systems that cannot be fully understood by mathematical analysis or simulations. Why is it that "simple" science does not apply to such natural phenomena? One reason is that in such phenomena, very small changes can produce very great changes — the so-called butterfly effect. The butterfly effect gets its name from the following scenario: a butterfly in the Amazon rain forest flaps its wings. That tiny action becomes the starting point for an infinite chain of events, eventually resulting in a change in the global weather.

Endo: Sort of like the saying, "For want of a nail…the kingdom was lost."

Ikeda: Yes. That's a fine example of the time-tested wisdom of ordinary people. They knew that all things are intimately related.

Suda: Yes. But though the same butterfly may flap its wings the next day, it might have no effect on the weather at all. This uncertainty is one of the distinctive characteristics of the science of complexity. Another difference between the science of simplicity and the science of complexity is clearly demonstrated in the difference between the workings of a computer and the human brain. Computers are excellent at mathematical computations, processing data and storing large amounts of information, but if even the smallest error enters the data, it can impede proper function.

The human brain, on the other hand, is not well-suited for such large computations or processing or memorizing huge volumes of information, but it has a flexibility that allows it to deal with what would correspond to small errors in data, as well as an ability to extract in a moment the information it needs from a wide variety of sources. A computer programmed to play chess, no matter how sophisticated it is, often loses to a human player.

Ikeda: Even this brief overview shows that modern science is gradually coming into harmony with the Lotus Sutra's teaching of the true aspect of all phenomena. What is crucial is to direct this tendency toward a recognition of the infinite worth and nobility of the individual.

Saito: We need a science that doesn't alienate people but instead gives them inspiration and courage.

Ikeda: Yes. Learning must give people hope. What other use is there for knowledge? I am reminded of Lu Xun's lecture at the People's School of Xiamen University in China.

Suda: Lu Xun taught at Xiamen University for a short time, didn't he?

Ikeda: Yes. The People's School was a learning facility started by the students of Xiamen University for children of poor families. They took on the role of teachers and tried to teach children who would otherwise have few educational opportunities. Lu Xun had been invited to speak at the opening ceremony [in December 1926].

First, a certain high-ranking professor mounted the dais. There was no applause. Speaking on the significance of the People's School, he said: "This school will benefit the people because… because, for example, if servants can read, they will be able to please their masters by delivering their letters correctly."[9] It was a remark of unbelievable arrogance—a sign of blatant contempt for the common people. He was baldly declaring that the only reason for them to gain an education was to please their masters.

Seeing Lu Xun's burning gaze on him, the professor faltered, but blundered on: "Their masters will be pleased and hire them, and they will earn their daily bread."[10] Snickering arose in the auditorium. The professor was completely befuddled and fled from the podium. Then Lu Xun stood up to speak:

"What I want to say is this: You are all children of laborers and farmers. Because you are poor, you were deprived of the opportunity to study. But the only poverty you suffer is that of money. You are not poor in intelligence or ability. Though you may come from impoverished families, you are equal in intelligence and ability to all others."[11]

Lu Xun glanced at the professor and the university president sitting in the front row, who by now had broken out in a cold sweat. Then he turned back to the students.

"No one is so powerful," he continued, "that he is free to treat you as his eternal slave…. Nor is it your fate to remain poor all your lives." His voice rose. "If only you have the determination, if only you have the will to fight, you will definitely succeed, you will definitely have a bright future."[12] The auditorium was rocked with thunderous applause.

Endo: What a moving story!

Ikeda: Lu Xun wanted to let his listeners know that all people, no matter what their circumstances, are equal and have unlimited potential. And he wanted to encourage them never to give up, no matter what temporal powers or what fate might stand in their way. He urged them to overcome any such obstacle, to rise to the challenge and triumph.

Saito: When you think about it, Shakyamuni's original intent in teaching the true aspect of all phenomena was to urge us all to rise to the same challenge. And Shakyamuni himself took the lead and fought that battle as well. The "Expedient Means" chapter states:

> I view things through the Buddha eye,
> I see the living beings in the six paths,
> how poor and distressed they are, without
>   merit or wisdom,
> how they enter the perilous road of birth and death,
> their sufferings continuing with never a break,...
> [they] enter deeply into erroneous views,
> hoping to shed suffering through greater suffering.
> For the sake of these living beings
> I summon up a mind of great compassion. (LS2, 42)

Ikeda: Compassion means to feel others' sufferings as our own. It originates from a deep inner cry of sympathy when we share someone's pain. Shakyamuni sought a way to free all living beings from the chains of suffering, and he agonized and fought to perfect that way. In "Expedient Means," he declares: "I have come into this impure and evil world" (LS2, 44).

With this thought, Shakyamuni resolved to take up the challenge of leading others to enlightenment. Great people stand tall in the center of the storm. It is only by facing the challenges of a chaotic world that we can test our mettle. And the heart of one who fights against all odds is filled with compassion as vast as the ocean for future generations.

A student of Xiamen University even remarked to Lu Xun as they made their way to the ceremony, "When I am near you, I feel refreshed and energized, as if I were actually next to the ocean."

"No," replied Lu Xun and pointed to the laborers' children who were joyfully entering the building, "there is your ocean."[13]

Endo: The Lotus Sutra has often been likened to the great ocean, hasn't it?

Ikeda: Yes. Nichiren Daishonin writes, "[The Lotus Sutra] is like the water of the great ocean, a single drop of which contains water from all the countless streams and rivers" (WND, 69). The whole is included in the parts. All the treasures of the universe are there in each individual. The drama of infinite value-creation begins with the actions of one person.

Saito: The English philosopher Alfred North Whitehead taught that nature was not a conglomeration of things but a series of events. He writes: "Life can only be understood as an aim at that perfection which the conditions of its environment allow. But the aim is always beyond the attained fact."[14] In other words, life aims for perfection, always seeking to approach it as closely as possible. It is always trying to transcend the attained fact, the present reality.

Ikeda: That may be true. Life is not some simple mechanism governed only by physical laws of cause and effect. Of course, since living things are made of matter, they do have a mechanical aspect. But they are not simply machines and nothing more. All life has a fundamental desire to create value. Value is a relative notion, and in this world, this tapestry of relationships, life is always seeking to create ever better relationships, that is, ever greater value.

Life tries to weave a more beautiful tapestry (the value of beauty), a more useful tapestry (the value of benefit), a better tapestry (the value of good). I think there can be no doubt that creating value is a very important characteristic. In that sense, the struggle to achieve perfection is proof of life.

Life aspires toward a perfection that is "always beyond the attained fact." From the perspective of the mutual possession of the Ten Worlds, all life, whatever its present form, is seeking to transcend its present state in pursuit of perfection.

The essential nature of life is to aspire for the perfection that is the state of Buddhahood. This aspiration is expressed in a passage that appears throughout the sutra: "pressing their palms together and turning toward the Buddha." In other words, all life, at the most fundamental level, seeks the Buddha.

The teaching of the true aspect of all phenomena, I think, reveals this truth that every living thing is an irreplaceably precious existence. Nichiren Daishonin proclaimed this essence of the Lotus Sutra for all to hear. And in modern times, the same message was proclaimed by Mr. Makiguchi and Mr. Toda, who directly inherited the Daishonin's spirit.

After Mr. Makiguchi's death in prison, Mr. Toda composed this poem in his cell:

> *I clutch in my hand the wish-granting jewel,*
> *My heart cries out, "With this,*
> *I will save everyone!"*
> *My mentor smiles in peace.*

The "wish-granting jewel" refers to the principle of three thousand realms in a single moment of life; it refers to the Gohonzon. In the Gosho, we find, "'Precious jewel' stands for the principle of three thousand realms in a single moment of life" (GZ, 741). Faith based on this principle means being absolutely confident that, by one's very presence, it is possible to change everything. It is faith propelled by a "stand alone" spirit.

Now is the time for every individual practitioner to fully display the limitless power of the Mystic Law. For the entire Soka Gakkai exists in each individual. In each individual, the entire twenty-first century awaits. That is why I hope all of our members, without exception, will carry out their precious missions— missions that each was born to fulfill in this lifetime.

That fighting spirit, that determination to keep challenging oneself, is itself the soul of victory, the power source that will allow each person to create a glorious decade in this important stage of our movement.

NOTES

1. *Profound Meaning of the Lotus Sutra* (Hokke Gengi), vol. 2.

2. William Blake, "Auguries of Innocence."

3. *Toda Josei Zenshu* (The Collected Works of Josei Toda).

4. *Great Concentration and Insight.*

5. *Toda Josei Zenshu.*

6. This and all following quotations in this paragraph are from: Albert Einstein, *The World As I See It*, trans. Alan Harris (London: Watts & Company, 1935), p. 56.

7. Albert Einstein, *Out of My Later Years* (New York: The Philosophical Library, Inc., 1950), p. 29.

8. Ibid., p. 27.

9. Translated from the Japanese: *LuXun, Rojin no Shogai* (The Life of Lu Xun), trans. Jiro Kaneko and Shin'ichi Ohara (Tokyo: Toho Shoten, 1978), p. 82.

10. Ibid., p. 83.

11. Ibid., p. 84.

12. Ibid.

13. Ibid.

14. Quoted in Charles Birch, *The Liberation of Life* (Cambridge: Cambridge University Press, 1981), p. 108.

Glossary

bodhisattva (Skt) A being who aspires to attain Buddhahood and carries out altruistic practices to achieve that goal. Compassion predominates in bodhisattvas, who postpone their own entry into nirvana in order to lead others toward enlightenment.

Bodhisattvas of the Earth Those who chant and propagate Nam-myoho-renge-kyo. *Earth* indicates the enlightened nature of all people. The term describes the innumerable bodhisattvas who appear in the "Emerging from the Earth" chapter of the Lotus Sutra and are entrusted by Shakyamuni with the task of propagating the Law after his passing. In several of his writings, Nichiren Daishonin identifies his own role with that of their leader, Bodhisattva Superior Practices.

consistency from beginning to end The last of the ten factors mentioned in the "Expedient Means" chapter of the Lotus Sutra. It is the integrating factor that unifies the other nine in every moment of life.

daimoku (Jpn) Literally, 'title.' 1) The title of a sutra, in particular the title of the Lotus Sutra, Myoho-renge-kyo. 2) The invocation of Nam-myoho-renge-kyo in Nichiren Daishonin's Buddhism.

Daishonin (Jpn) Literally, 'great sage.' In particular, this honorific title is applied to Nichiren to show reverence for him as the

Buddha who appears in the Latter Day of the Law to save all humankind.

devil king of the sixth heaven   The king of devils, who dwells in the highest of the six heavens of the world of desire. He works to obstruct Buddhist practice and delights in sapping the life force of other beings. He is also regarded as the manifestation of the fundamental darkness inherent in life. Also called the heavenly devil.

Eagle Peak (Skt Gridhrakuta)   Also, Vulture Peak. A mountain located to the northeast of Rajagriha, the capital of Magadha in ancient India, where Shakyamuni is said to have expounded the Lotus Sutra. Eagle Peak also symbolizes the Buddha land or the state of Buddhahood. In this sense, the 'pure land of Eagle Peak' is often used.

Gohonzon   *Go* means 'worthy of honor' and *honzon* means 'object of fundamental respect.' The object of devotion in Nichiren Daishonin's Buddhism and the embodiment of the Mystic Law permeating all phenomena. It takes the form of a mandala inscribed on paper or on wood with characters representing the Mystic Law as well as the Ten Worlds, including Buddhahood. Nichiren Daishonin's Buddhism holds that all people possess the Buddha nature and can attain Buddhahood through faith in the Gohonzon.

gongyo   Literally, 'assiduous practice.' In the Daishonin's Buddhism, it means to chant Nam-myoho-renge-kyo and portions of the "Expedient Means" and "Life Span" chapters of the Lotus Sutra. It is performed morning and evening.

Gosho   Literally, 'honored writings.' The individual and collected writings of Nichiren Daishonin.

human revolution   A concept coined by the Soka Gakkai's second president, Josei Toda, to indicate the self-reformation of
an individual — the strengthening of life force and the establishment of Buddhahood — that is the goal of Buddhist
practice.

kalpa   (Skt) An extremely long period of time. Sutras and treatises differ in their definitions, but kalpas fall into two major
categories, those of measurable and immeasurable duration.
There are three kinds of measurable kalpas: small, medium
and major. One explanation sets the length of a small kalpa
at approximately sixteen million years. According to Buddhist cosmology, a world repeatedly undergoes four stages:
formation, continuance, decline and disintegration. Each of
these four stages lasts for twenty small kalpas and is equal to
one medium kalpa. Finally, one complete cycle forms a major
kalpa.

kosen-rufu   Literally, to 'widely declare and spread [Buddhism].'
Nichiren Daishonin defines Nam-myoho-renge-kyo of the
Three Great Secret Laws as the law to be widely declared
and spread during the Latter Day. There are two aspects of
kosen-rufu: the kosen-rufu of the entity of the Law, or the
establishment of the Dai-Gohonzon, which is the basis of
the Three Great Secret Laws; and the kosen-rufu of sub-
stantiation, the widespread acceptance of faith in the Dai-
Gohonzon among the people.

ku   A fundamental Buddhist concept, variously translated as nonsubstantiality, emptiness, void, latency, relativity, etc. The concept that entities have no fixed or independent nature.

Latter Day of the Law   Also, the Latter Day. The last of the
three periods following Shakyamuni Buddha's death when

Buddhism falls into confusion and Shakyamuni's teachings lose the power to lead people to enlightenment. A time when the essence of the Lotus Sutra will be propagated to save all humankind.

Lotus Sutra   The highest teaching of Shakyamuni Buddha, it reveals that all people can attain enlightenment and declares that his former teachings should be regarded as preparatory.

mahasattva   A 'great being.' Another term for bodhisattva.

Mystic Law   The ultimate law of life and the universe. The law of Nam-myoho-renge-kyo.

Nam-myoho-renge-kyo   The ultimate law of the true aspect of life permeating all phenomena in the universe. The invocation established by Nichiren Daishonin on April 28, 1253. Nichiren Daishonin teaches that this phrase encompasses all laws and teachings within itself, and that the benefit of chanting Nam-myoho-renge-kyo includes the benefit of conducting all virtuous practices. *Nam* means 'devotion to'; *myoho* means 'Mystic Law'; *renge* refers to the lotus flower, which simultaneously blooms and seeds, indicating the simultaneity of cause and effect; *kyo* means sutra, the teaching of a Buddha.

Nichiren Daishonin   The thirteenth-century Japanese Buddhist teacher and reformer who taught that all people have the potential for enlightenment. He defined the universal Law as Nam-myoho-renge-kyo and established the Gohonzon as the object of devotion for all people to attain Buddhahood. Daishonin is an honorific title that means 'great sage.'

Mahayana   One of two main branches of Buddhism. It calls itself Mahayana or the 'Great Vehicle' because its teachings enable all beings to attain Buddhahood. It lays particular emphasis upon the bodhisattva.

oneness of body and mind   A principle explaining that the two seemingly distinct phenomena of body, or the physical aspect of life, and mind, or its spiritual aspect, are two integral phases of the same entity.

Shakyamuni   Also, Siddhartha Gautama. Born in India (present-day southern Nepal) about three thousand years ago, he is the first recorded Buddha and founder of Buddhism. For fifty years, he expounded various sutras (teachings), culminating in the Lotus Sutra.

Ten Worlds   Ten life-conditions that a single entity of life manifests.

Theravada   'Teaching of the Elders.' One of two main branches of Buddhism, together with Mahayana. It teaches that since Buddhahood is almost impossible to attain, one should aim for the lesser goal of arhat, or worthy. Emphasizes a strict adherence to discipline and a literal interpretation of doctrine.

three assemblies in two places   A division of the Lotus Sutra according to the location and sequence of the events described in it. The three assemblies are the first assembly on Eagle Peak, the Ceremony in the Air and the second assembly on Eagle Peak. The two places are on Eagle Peak and in the air.

three obstacles and four devils   Various obstacles and hindrances to the practice of Buddhism. The three obstacles are: 1) the obstacle of earthly desires; 2) the obstacle of karma, which may also refer to opposition from one's spouse or children;

and 3) the obstacle of retribution, also obstacles caused by one's superiors, such as rulers or parents. The four devils are: 1) the hindrance of the five components; 2) the hindrance of earthly desires; 3) the hindrance of death, because untimely death obstructs one's practice of Buddhism or because the premature death of another practitioner causes doubts; and 4) the hindrance of the devil king.

three thousand realms in a single moment of life   Also, *ichinen sanzen*. A philosophical system set forth by T'ien-t'ai in his *Great Concentration and Insight*, clarifying the mutually inclusive relationship of the ultimate truth and the phenomenal world. This means that the life of Buddhahood is universally inherent in all beings, and the distinction between a common person and a Buddha is a phenomenal one.

Thus Come One   One of the ten honorable titles for a Buddha, meaning one who has arrived from the world of truth. That is, the Buddha appears from the world of enlightenment and, as a person who embodies wisdom and compassion, leads other beings to enlightenment.

Index